Alfred Watkins' Herefordshire

Alfred Watkins' Herefordshire

in his own words and photographs

with a biographical introduction by
Ron & Jennifer Shoesmith

Logaston Press

A woman at the well at Wormsley Hill

LOGASTON PRESS
Little Logaston Woonton Almeley
Herefordshire HR3 6QH
www.logastonpress.co.uk

First published by Logaston Press 2012
Copyright © Ron and Jennifer Shoesmith

ISBN 978 1906663 67 4

Typeset in Garamond by Logaston Press
and printed in Malta by Gutenberg Press

Contents

Brockhampton – the gatehouse over the moat and the late 14th-century manor (now in the care of the National Trust)

Introduction

It must have been some 20 years ago, when my book *Alfred Watkins – A Herefordshire Man* was published, that I was given the manuscript of Alfred's unpublished book *The Masefield Country* (which was still in draft form when Alfred died in 1935) by his grandson, the late Felix Watkins, in the hope that at some time in the future it could be published. The typescript sat on the bookshelf for many years until my wife and I were encouraged by several people 'to do something about it'. This book is the result.

Alfred put his book together in the early 1930s, shortly after hearing John Masefield's speech accepting the Freedom of the City of Hereford in 1930. By that time Alfred had written several articles on the general subject – the area around Ledbury – for the *Transactions* of the Woolhope Naturalists' Field Club. The area was one that he knew exceptionally well: from working as an 'outrider' for his father's brewery and later for the family flour mills; from long walks along the Malvern Hills; from a canoe trip down the Hereford, Ledbury and Gloucester canal; and from conversations with the many people he met – people who worked the red earth of that part of Herefordshire and knew the countryside well. It is now some 80 years since Alfred wrote this book. In it he included reminiscences of conversations he had as a young man with elderly people whose memories went back to the early part of the 19th century – some 200 years ago.

The last chapter of *The Masefield Country*, 'The Soul of the Soil', brings out Alfred's basic philosophy – that those who work in close association with 'mother earth' are 'most of all in touch with, and understand, its soul'. To illustrate this sense of connection, he uses the work of three poets – William Langland, Elizabeth Barrett and John Masefield – all living at one time or another in the Ledbury area, which is described by Alfred as 'Laureate Land'. We are very grateful to the estate of John Masefield and the Society of Authors for permission to quote extensively from John Masefield's poetry in chapter 5 of *The Masefield Country*.

Several people helped to transform the original typescript into a publishable format. The first attempt was by Wendy Holton of Moreton on Lugg, who produced an easily readable format; she was followed by Karen Johnson of Logaston Press and my wife Jennifer, who put much time and effort into sorting out Alfred's many scribbled inserts and corrections. Without all their help, Alfred's final work would have lingered on the bookshelf for many more years. Thanks too to Alan Duncan for producing a map based on Alfred's key to the map he drew for the book, which has so far failed to surface. If anyone knows the whereabouts of the map or anything else relating to this text, we would be grateful to hear from you. In particular, along with his manuscript, Alfred left a list of the photographs to be included. We were unable to find original versions of those specified, and have used copies or similar photographs. Some we were unable to locate in any form. This made us wonder if Alfred collected together the glass plate negatives of the photographs he wanted to use, removing them from his collections, and if perhaps on his death they were not passed down his family with the manuscript (his photographs were willed elsewhere) but separated from it, and subsequently lost. If anyone has any knowledge of a collection of approximately thirty negatives or photographs which could be this set, the publishers would be delighted to hear from them.

This book is in three parts – an introductory biography of Alfred Watkins to set the scene; *The Masefield Country*; and a photographic section to show the diversity of Alfred's talent for and contribution to photography. All photographs are by Alfred Watkins unless otherwise credited. We would like to express our most grateful thanks to all who have helped and taken an interest in the production of this book, especially to Lauren Price and her colleagues at Hereford City Library for allowing us to include photographs from their Alfred Watkins collection, and to Andy and Karen of Logaston Press for their encouragement and great help throughout the project.

Ron Shoesmith
September 2012

The Wye at Hereford towards the end of the 19th century. The photograph is taken from upstream of the Wye Bridge and includes a small boathouse to the left of centre, where the modern Rowing Club building now stands.
Alfred was at one time the club captain.

Alfred Watkins –
A Herefordshire Man

by

Ron & Jennifer Shoesmith

1

Alfred's early life

Alfred Watkins' father, Charles Watkins, was of yeoman stock, being born to a small farmer in Mitcheldean, a small town on the edge of the Forest of Dean in Gloucestershire, on 21 January 1821. His parents were also apparently carriers, a trade which, in the period before the railways arrived, was of some considerable importance. His father would have used long, hooded wagons with teams of strong horses to transport countryside produce such as grain, wood and fruit to the markets. Their trade would have allowed the Watkins family a degree of independence uncommon in a rural community. One can perhaps assume that the younger members of the family had the rare luxury, virtually unknown outside the landed classes, of being able to travel in their father's wagons to places far outside the Forest. Charles continued in the same type of business for, as a young man, he drove coaches daily between Hereford and Cirencester.

It was to become landlord of the Three Crowns Inn in Eign Street (now an Amusement Arcade in Eign Gate) that Charles Watkins came to Hereford as a single man in 1840. Before he had been in the city very long, he found himself a wife, Ann Hill. She had been brought to Hereford from Ireland to work in one of the local inns and was thus hardly the ideal choice for an up-and-coming businessman. According to Peter Pocket, the one-time landlord of the British Camp Inn, who was an old friend of Charles and acted as best man, the wedding took place 'somewhere on the Gloucestershire border'. Peter, described in the 1870s as 'a quiet little man of the Ham Peggotty type of face', would not give

away any other details. Whatever else, the marriage was extremely successful, and it is clear that Ann Watkins overcame any prejudice that there may have been in Hereford society concerning her humble beginnings. Charles and Ann had two children, Charlotte and Charles, whilst they lived and worked at the Three Crowns.

In the late 1840s the family moved to the Imperial Inn in Widemarsh Street – not a large establishment, but one with potential, and Charles must have felt sure that he could improve the trade and thus make it the basis of his fortune. However, he continued to have an interest in the Three Crowns and was still shown as landlord there in the 1858 Kelly's *Directory*.

Whilst at the Imperial, Charles and Ann Watkins had a further eight children between 1847 and 1860, although the two youngest died in infancy from either diphtheria or typhoid. Apart from Charlotte and Charles, Ann, John and Henry were also older than Alfred. He was born on 27 January 1855, the sixth of the eight surviving children, and had two younger sisters, Fanny and Alice. In the middle part of the 19th century the Imperial Inn was very different to the present Imperial Hotel. It was much smaller, occupying only the southern third of the ground on which the present building stands. A late 19th-century description gives some indication of the building where Alfred spent the first few years of his life. It contained a smoke room and a large public bar that had no less than four entrances. To the rear were the kitchen, the back kitchen and a spirit store, whilst in the basement there were stock rooms and a beer cellar. On the first floor they had a large sitting room and, at the rear, two bedrooms. The second floor contained additional attic bedrooms. At that time it may well have been lit by gas, for a gas works had been built in the city in 1836.

Behind the building was a long, narrow yard approached from Widemarsh Street through an archway. The yard contained the

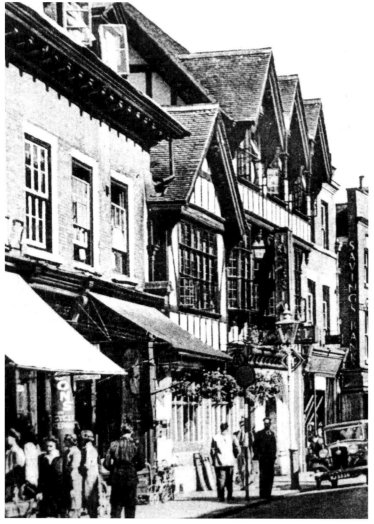

The Imperial Inn in the 1930s with the Mansion House to the left

brewhouse and other sheds and it was here that Charles Watkins produced the various brews that not only made his reputation with native Herefordians, but also were the start of his fortune. Many years later Alfred, in a letter to the *Hereford Times,* wrote:

> My father told me that a great deal of beer went into the making of that tunnel [the railway tunnel under Dinmore Hill], and as he had just built his new brewery (he had been up to the Great Exhibition of 1851, and there bought the newest brewing appliances, glorified under the high-sounding name of 'Imperial patent' thus providing a name for his inn, and for the larger brewery he built later) he came into most of the supplying.

The educational system in the middle of the 19th century operated at two different levels; first there were the charity schools and those attached to the parishes and supported by the various churches. But in addition there was a gradually increasing number of private, fee-paying schools, both day and boarding. Alfred was sent to one of the latter which was conveniently situated in what was until recently the Farmers Club at the junction of Widemarsh Street and Blueschool Street.

This fine timber-framed building was built in the late 15th or early 16th century. At the beginning of the 19th century it was in use as a ladies' school being run by a Miss Croucher. She employed the famous artist, David Cox, for some time as a drawing master at a salary of £100 *per annum*. In 1865 it was re-established as a boys school by the Reverend W. Bowell M.A., so Alfred must have been one of its first pupils. He was not impressed by it at all, for many years later he told his son that it was 'a shocking bad school where the teaching was perfectly dreadful and I learned absolutely nothing'. However, he appears to have taken an early and extensive interest in the building, for he noted during a visit in 1920, some fifty years after he had been a pupil there, that one of the rooms that was then bare had been panelled when he was at school.

The Widemarsh Street gatehouse where Alfred went to school. Later it became the Farmers Club, recently closed. (Ken Hoverd, 1990)

Whilst Alfred was still very young, his father extended his brewing interests and bought the then defunct Hereford Brewery, on the opposite side of Bewell Street to the rear entry of the Three Crowns (the brewery was where the Tesco supermarket now stands). Transferring his brewing interests from the Imperial Inn, Charles re-named his new purchase the Imperial Brewery.

Although there have been some improvements in this narrow street in recent times, it does not appear to have ever had any great character of its own. Appearances are deceptive, however, and

The main thoroughfare through the Imperial Brewery looking north from Bewell Street. The large building with the chimney is the brewhouse and on the right is the vat room. (From *Hereford Illustrated* 1892)

The 'Stews' off Bewell Street, which dated to the 16th century and were demolished just after the First World War

Holmer Park, the house designed and built by Charles Watkins, shortly after it was completed (Bustin, Hereford)

in the mid-19th century, when Alfred Watkins was a young boy walking from his home in the Imperial Inn to his father's other inn and his newly-acquired brewery, Bewell Street would have been much more full of interest than it is now. There were several well-established inns including the Rummer Tavern, the Weavers Arms, the Royal Standard (later called the Pippin) and the Bowling Green – the latter being the only one to survive to the present day. There were also many small businesses that would attract a youngster's attention, including a shoemaker, a candlemaker, a tailor and a clockmaker, not to mention several dining rooms. In addition, leading off the street to the north were narrow passages which opened out into several courts, such as Sheriffs Court and Fryers Court, containing small half-timbered houses, demolished many years ago as part of a slum clearance programme. Many years later, when there was a proposal to change the name of the street, Alfred wrote to the *Hereford Times*:

> It has always been a mean street, but it was an adjoining lane which had an especially unsavoury reputation, and this, the city fathers, without the faintest result, tried to sweeten by calling it another name. Now even supposing (I don't say it is) that a nest of sinners is to be found in Bewell Street, the fact won't be altered by calling it All Saints Street.

As owner of one of the principal breweries in the city, Charles needed an appropriate residence and it was during the 1860s that he decided to design and build his own house. This was Holmer Park, now on the outskirts of Hereford but then well in the country although sufficiently close to the city for convenience. Rather than buy bricks he dug his own clay pits in the grounds, later utilizing the area as a sunken rose garden. The iron railings which frame what is now the rear gated entrance onto Church Way were originally part of the churchyard railings around St. Paul's Cathedral. Charles acquired them on one of his occasional visits to London, when he found they were being replaced. These railings are thought to have been made of 'wealdon iron' from the local ore in the Weald in Sussex. Very few examples survive to the present day.

One of Alfred's earliest memories concerned the demolition of the Market Hall in High Town in 1862, when he was barely seven. He mentions the 'dim but vivid memory of the clustered columns' in his *Guide to the Old House* published in 1934. In its time the Market Hall was one of the most important and impressive buildings in the whole of the county, standing on a raised, stone-flagged floor. When it was built, in the latter part of the 16th century, it was three storeys high, standing on 27 wooden columns with an open ground floor for the market. At the end of the 18th century the top floor was deemed unsafe and the building was reduced to a two-storey edifice which was then stuccoed, thus losing much of its elevational splendour. Although plans were prepared for its restoration these came to nought and the building was finally demolished, being sold to William Davies of Widemarsh Street for £200. Its position and size can still be appreciated by the visitor to High Town, for its shape is still outlined by a dark stone edging in the paving.

Charles took the opportunity to purchase parts of the Market Hall to use in the garden of his new house. The timbers, which included four pillars and several decorated spandrels, were re-used to make an aviary close to the Church Way entry to Holmer Park. Now a listed building, this small memory of what was once the

The Market Hall in High Town, Hereford, in the mid-19th century, after it had had its upper storey removed

Posts and spandrels belonging to Hereford's Market Hall, re-erected as an aviary at Holmer Park, later to become a summer house.

Charles Watkins with gun, dog and game on the steps at
Holmer Park in about 1870 (Bustin, Hereford)

pride of High Town can still be seen on the side of Church Way, the
minor road leading eastwards off the A49 a short distance north of
the Roman Road junction. Holmer Park was until recently Inco-
Alloys' social club and is now a spa and health club.

Another childhood memory, involving one of the most historic
sites in the city, emerged in an article Alfred wrote in 1933 when
he was 78 years old. There he discussed the story of an under-
ground passage, possibly associated with Hereford Castle, which
was reputed to have been visible in the river bank in the latter part
of the 19th century close to where the Victoria Suspension Bridge
(built in 1898) now stands. He demonstrated that this supposed
passage was actually a large culvert – the old outlet for the stream
which once encircled the castle and fed the castle mill. He then
went on to say that

> My knowledge of the spot goes further back to my
> childhood recollection of scrambling down the then
> gully here and over the ruined walls and foundation
> of the ancient Castle Mill, then being demolished.
> This must have been about 1861. It was in 1863 that I
> heard the Russian gun fired on the marriage-day of the
> Princess Alexandra, being present in the Castle Green,
> and remember running off behind Hogg's Mount to
> escape the terrible hurt to the drums of my young ears,
> for the concussion broke many windows at the Hospital.
> The site of the Castle Mill was not that of the Hospital
> Lodge, as usually stated, but low down in the trough of
> the stream running from the mill pool or moat, as clearly
> shown on Speed's map.

From this it is apparent that Alfred was climbing about the Castle
Mill ruins, close by the river bank, at the tender age of six. His
memory of these early events never deserted him, and some 70
years later he was still able to provide vivid images of the things he
saw as a child.

Circumstances changed for Charles Watkins in 1870 when
an unexpected opportunity arose to buy Bewell House – a large,

mid-18th-century mansion in its own grounds at the western end of Bewell Street adjoining the Imperial Brewery. It appears that he kept this building as his town house for many years, whilst spending much time at his various properties in the countryside. Alfred recalled that he had lived in Bewell House as a lad, but apparently for no great length of time. The building eventually became the brewery manager's house.

In the latter part of the 19th century Bewell House would have been a very impressive town house for the Watkins family. The main floor included a breakfast room, a library, a drawing room and a dining room, together with a servants' hall, kitchen, scullery, butler's pantry and the usual services. There were four principal bedrooms on the first floor and a further four on the second. The forecourt onto Bewell Street contained stabling which included two stalls, a loose box and a coach house with a loft above. Behind the house much of the formal garden was retained, although the eastern part (and later the northern part) was walled off and taken over by the expanding brewery. This was a far cry indeed from the limited accommodation at the old Imperial Inn. Bewell House is still a significant part of the streetscape in this part of Hereford, having both preceded and outlived the brewery. It is a II* listed building now used as offices.

To the west of Bewell House there was some vacant ground (now lost to the inner relief road), and this was where Charles decided to diversify. He built St. George's Hall, a substantial brick building some 85 feet long and 65 feet wide with a gallery and a slate roof. It was designed as a roller-skating rink to cater for growing demand during one of the earliest crazes for this sport. One wonders how much the father was influenced by the wishes of his young children in this enterprise, for it is known that Alfred, at least, became somewhat of an expert. It was in 1879 that St. George's Hall became the first building in the city to be lit by electric light. The bulbs, being blue, caused considerable merriment in the city since the Watkins family were known to be supporters of the Liberal, Gladstone. When the craze for roller-skating diminished (and the Watkins children grew up) the building was used for

St. George's Hall – once a skating rink – after the fire

some time as a hall for travelling entertainers but, as the expanding brewery required even more room, it was taken over and became first the hop and ale store and then the mineral water factory. The whole building was eventually destroyed by a fire. Its final use was as a garage and depot for coaches.

Alfred's other sports were rowing and swimming, and he was a member of the Hereford Rowing Club. He took part in many events and eventually became the club captain. As a young man, Alfred served in the Herefordshire Volunteers, which had been formed during the Napoleonic Wars. It was under the control of Colonel Heywood of Hope End in Colwall parish, near the border with Worcestershire, an area that Alfred often visited and which is the subject of his final book.

Charles was a typical Victorian entrepreneur and his various businesses expanded rapidly. They must also have been very profitable, for shortly after 1870 he decided to move further out into

Wisteston Chapel from the north-west shortly before it was demolished in 1909

In the courtyard at Wisteston Court. This was the home of the Watkins family from about 1870, but has since been demolished

the countryside and bought the Wisteston Court Estate in the parish of Marden, some six miles north of Hereford. The estate was substantial and he is listed in the various Directories of the period as 'a hop-grower and farmer'. The Court included a timber-framed 15th-century wing, which probably started its life as an open hall, as well as much 17th-century work and, together with the Hereford Market Hall, may have served as an introduction to architectural history for the young Alfred. Wisteston Court has since been lost – it was already in poor condition when the Royal Commission on Ancient Monuments visited in 1930 and continued to deteriorate during the war years. It was derelict in 1963 when Pevsner included it in his *Buildings of Herefordshire* and now all that remains is a pile of rubble.

Close to the Court was Wisteston Chapel, once belonging to the preceptory of Dinmore (Knights Hospitallers), but afterwards acquired by the proprietor of the Court who appointed chaplains to perform the service. The chapel was rebuilt in about 1715 and restored in 1860. When Charles and his family moved to Wisteston, a service was held in the Chapel for about six Sundays in the summer. Alfred recollected that:

It was a quaint Queen Anne interior, with coved plaster ceiling, oak panelled wainscot, and high oak pews, the highest, the Court pew near the door, in which we as children could crouch down out of sight. ... In a few years the six services dwindled to two or three and soon ceased for all time. ... The chapel began to decay, and at my father's death in 1888 he left by will £25 towards a fund for its repair.

Repairs did not happen, and in the spring of 1909 the Chapel was demolished without any record being taken.

By the late 1870s Charles had bought yet another property, Little Burlton Farm at Burghill, where he is shown in a Directory as 'farmer and landowner'.

By 1879 Charles and Ann had made their final move to Wilcroft in Hagley, then part of Lugwardine parish, some four miles east of Hereford, although he still kept the Wisteston Court Estate. Wilcroft was an 18th-century mansion of considerable character which Charles extended to provide the accommodation he needed both for his large family and for his requirements as a major businessman in the city. The building still survives, but

Wilcroft (Ken Hoverd, 1990)

Ann Watkins at Wilcroft in about 1897 when she was 76

has since been split into smaller, separate dwellings. He may well have moved there to be closer to his son John, who lived at the nearby Pomona Farm in Withington parish. Charles was struck with paralysis in 1885 whilst visiting Llandrindod Wells, and from that time onwards was rendered helpless and speechless although he retained his other faculties. He eventually died in 1888.

Charles' will is a rather complex document. He appears to have tried to ensure that each child had a similar share of the estate, but because he had already passed on to his sons various properties and business interests, he seems to have tried to make things equal by making some of the sons pay to the estate something for their individual inheritance. The one thing that does stand out is that he expected the male heirs to look after their mother during her life and also their sisters. The monies paid by the sons to the estate by way of purchase or rent provided the annual income for the females in the family and then, on their mother's death, everything left over was to be sold and divided equally between all the children. Alfred appears to have inherited half a business (the Imperial Flour Mills) and several properties, the remaining half being left to his brother Charles, assuming that they could work together, as in fact they did. However, each had the option to sell his own half.

2

The family businesses

Charles Watkins' first main acquisition in about 1858 was the Hereford Brewery. It was a brave move, for the brewery, founded in 1834, had been closed for some 12 years. Using his expertise from the Imperial Inn, Charles was able to increase his output substantially and rapidly extended the premises by adding adequate stores for his already large wine and spirit business. It was then that he changed the name from the rather parochial Hereford Brewery to the much more impressive Imperial Brewery.

Alfred's elder brother, Henry, had already started to work in the brewery, and it must have been shortly after the family's move to Bewell House that Charles decided that Alfred should also learn the brewery business – inevitably by starting at the bottom. At a much later date, he remembered his early years at the brewery in an entertaining article in the *Hereford Times* about the blacksmith's craft.

> As a boy, with the run of my father's brewery, it was in the cooper's and blacksmith shops that I found my spiritual home. The first-named was perhaps in early days the most attractive, with its varied and strange craft-work and sweet smell of oak-chips and shavings. But in this place, where staves were shaved, bellied and trussed up, sharp cutting tools not to be trusted to small boys, were all about, and it was the same with the rather sterner guardian in the carpenter's domain.
>
> So, as I now know, it was the blacksmith's forge that laid the deepest spell on the mind of a young tool-user,

for not so easily damaged were the hammers and tongs, cold chisels and punches, and the 'Old Cole' who only occasionally had a smithy job to vary his regular engine driving, allowed a little lad to blow up the shred of fire on the hearth, to heat a bit of iron, and hammer it up into any kind of odd shape. And later on the friendly old man put me on to making my apprentice's pair of tongs.

A little later he probably worked in the coopers' shop, making casks from the native oak for he described this later:

> There were in the yard great open stacks, like chimneys some twenty-five feet high, of cleft English oak put to season for the coopers to make into casks. The woodmen cleft and sawed them in the rough the right sizes for staves and heads of kilderkins and barrels, each piled in its own stack – delightful for a boy to climb up inside!

Indeed, one of his first hobbies was the craft of woodworking for which he had considerable talent. It was an interest even mentioned in his obituary where it was said that surviving pieces showed a high standard of taste and skill. One wonders where these pieces are nowadays.

It was about 1873 when Alfred, then a young man of 18, started work as an outrider (the local word for a traveller), taking orders from country pubs for the expanding Imperial Brewery. His mode of transport during these early years was a horse and gig.

The coopers' shed at the Imperial Brewery where Alfred learnt how to work with wood

This must have been one of the most pleasant and leisurely ways of travelling around the countryside, being sufficiently slow to see and appreciate everything in the surrounding hills and fields. The horse would doubtless have needed little encouragement to stop, whilst, from his later writings, it is clear that Alfred needed even less inducement. In the *Hereford Times* in 1927, he mentions the old coach road from Hereford to Leominster, where it passed over Dinmore Hill. Writing as an observer, he commented that:

> On this road, if you look on the face of a rock, on the left before you get to the dangerous bend – (year after year a blue tit built her nest here when I was a lad) – you will see that old travellers have recorded their passing. 'No more this way' is one, and we wonder why L.M., who cut his record on Jan. 2nd, 1829, ceased passing, for another traveller I knew, who drove over the hill once a month calling at the inns for his father's brewery, also cut his full name half a century ago (in 1876), but could only do one letter a month, his nag being restive, so it took a year to finish. And this traveller is still occasionally 'on the road' doing trade journeys.

It would seem that Alfred did not find the brewery business very congenial, for he seems to have spent much of the time during his travels talking to people he met on the road irrespective of their status. He must also have taken every opportunity to examine churches, castles and other historic buildings when he visited the more remote parts of Herefordshire, in preference to selling his father's beer in the back-street public houses of the small county towns of Leominster, Ledbury, Kington and Ross.

After a few years of travelling for the brewery business, Alfred changed to working for the family's new flour mills. This was a business that was to give much more scope for his creative flair. The flour mills had been set up by Charles Watkins in about 1876, having taken over premises in Friars Street which had been originally built by a Captain Radford in 1834 as the Hereford Foundry. The enterprise had failed, and Charles Watkins bought the existing

Alfred's name, which he carved on a rock at Dinmore Hill at the rate of one letter a month during 1876

buildings and built onto them a new flour mill with six pairs of stones. This was to become the Imperial Flour Mills with an associated set of maltings. According to his daughter, Alfred 'after passing his miller's examinations was established as a partner in the family mill which, with shares in one of the family hotels [probably the Green Dragon in Broad Street] gave him an adequate living'.

When Alfred transferred to the milling business, he continued to travel around the Herefordshire countryside, but now visited the outlying farms rather than the back-street hostelries. The flour mills also gave him scope to try out his powers as an innovator and inventor. When he began working there, the mill was making use of the traditional millstones, operated by steam power, for grinding the grain. This was a laborious and time-consuming operation in a dark and gloomy factory building, probably lit by gas. Within a year of his joining the business, the young Alfred had made his first change. He arranged for the mill to be lighted by incandescent electric lamps served by a dynamo that had been moved from St. George's Hall. This would not just have been a factory improvement, it would have created a tremendous impression throughout

The Imperial Flour Mill early in the 20th century. The building on the left was the original foundry. For many years there was a spur off the main railway line at Barton Station to the mill.

Making doughmeters in 1913

the city, demonstrating the modern nature of the mill and the undoubted energy of the proprietor. It would also have provided impetus for the eventual introduction of electric light throughout the city.

But Alfred was not content with this single innovation – he wanted to ensure that the mill was the most efficient in the county. By 1882, he decided that the old grinding stones had to go and be replaced with a roller-milling plant, which he planned and erected. But his interest spread to all corners of the business, for he was studying every aspect of milling during these early years, and in 1883 he won the premier silver medal in the City and Guilds examination.

It was not long before he invented and obtained a patent for a specialized baker's thermometer. This was essentially a simple thermometer, but with a second scale which established the necessary heat of the liquor (for making up the dough), having first found the temperature of the flour. The calculation made on the scale of the instrument was, according to the instructions, 'based on a two-year's series of trials in an average bake-house'.

A second piece of apparatus was much more complex and an excellent example of Alfred's inventive flair. This was the dough-meter, brought out in two different patented forms – the bell-doughmeter and the more refined clock-doughmeter. Its purpose was to establish the correct length of time between starting the yeast and putting the bread in the oven. This was something that the baker had done previously only by experience. Alfred, as he also did in the photographic fields of exposure and development, aimed to put this on a scientific footing. In the instructions he wrote:

> The doughmeter does not supersede the baker's experience, but gives him a new and accurate power of gauging when his fermentation has attained just the result suited to his trade. It is to dough-making what a speedometer is to a motor car driver.

Loading the steam wagon at the Watkins' Imperial Flour Mills in 1905

Alfred's interest in baking bread continued for many years and in the 1890s he entered the long-running argument over white versus wholemeal flour. His son reported, much later, that Alfred had taken a miller's attitude to the question, condemning and discarding the wheat husks (the roughage, or what he called the 'offal') as being detrimental to the quality of a good loaf, but managing to retain the wheat germ.

The upper part of a Watkins doughmeter in Hereford City Museum (Ken Hoverd, 1990)

The winning Vagos loaf at one of the bakers' competitions

Thus, the Watkins' mill produced a wholemeal flour which would give a light, spongy, flavoursome loaf. This soon became popular far beyond the borders of Herefordshire. Indeed, the business acumen of the mill's owners was demonstrated when they organised a big competition for bakers producing the best loaf using the new flour, with a nice cheque and publicity for the winner. Alfred named the loaf 'Vagos' because the flour was milled at Hereford in the valley of the river Wye – named Vaga by the Romans.

By the beginning of the 20th century, Alfred's elder brother, Charles, had retired from the business and Alfred took on a new partner. This was E.S. Newman, an exceptionally able miller, interested and capable of increasing efficiency and making the works more profitable. The Vagos bread was only a part of the mill's output, and under Newman's efficiency drive, its sales were allowed to dwindle and finally cease completely. Although production ceased, the formula was kept for many years, finally to be lost, according to Alfred's son Allen, when an aged clerk, who kept all the firm's books, suddenly died of a heart attack. All that is left is Alfred's photograph of the winning loaf at one of the competitions! The mill continued to operate into the middle of the 20th century when the business closed down. Following a fire a few years ago, the buildings were all demolished and the site was redeveloped for housing.

The Watkins boys were all probably expected to learn the brewing trade, but it is apparent that not all of them had the same interest. Thus it was in 1883 that Charles Watkins decided to admit Alfred's older brother, Henry (who was reputed to be very clever), into partnership with him at the Imperial Brewery, and from that time on the son managed the entire brewery. However, he only survived his father by about a year, for in January 1889 he was found drowned in the River Lugg at Lugwardine.

The lack of any great interest in the brewery business by the remaining proprietors, Alfred and his older brother Charles, came to a head in 1898. The decision was made to sell by auction – the catalogue shows that, besides the brewery there were 35 hotels, public and beer houses in the city and neighbourhood and branches in Birmingham, Cardiff and Swansea. The reason for the sale, which took place in London, was stated to be that the propri-

The grinding stones in the Imperial Flour Mills in the latter part of the 19th century

The Hereford Brewery offices in Eign Street at the end of the 19th century. The ornate building is partly hidden by the extensive advertising boards. The building, now without the boards, still survives and through it runs the passageway leading to Tesco's supermarket.

etors 'were desirous of retiring' – at that time Alfred was 43 years old! The total sales of the brewery for the period 1895-7 averaged £36,160 10s. The Hereford Public Library copy of the sale particulars is annotated in ink with the comment '£64,000 highest bid for the lot'.

After varying uses, all the buildings that once comprised the Hereford Imperial Brewery were demolished by the early 1960s; the vast cellars being filled with rubble and the whole area being turned into a car park, with Bewell House, Charles Watkins' old home, standing rather forlorn in the middle. It was not until 1981, when a large area to the east (which had become a jam factory after the demolition of the slum housing) became available, that there was sufficient room to build the Tesco supermarket that now occupies the whole site, apart from the restored Bewell House, which is now used as offices.

3

Family life

Whilst brother Henry managed the brewery business until his death in 1889, Alfred and his older brother Charles continued to look after the flour mills. Brother John stayed out of the family businesses and became a farmer at Pomona Farm in Withington. By 1890, two years after his father died, John is also shown in directories as the owner of the Wisteston Court Estate but, like Henry, he also died relatively young.

Alfred's oldest sister, Charlotte, never married – as so often happened in large families, she probably spent most of her childhood years helping to look after the younger children during her mother's many pregnancies and, as she grew up, looking after her parents as they grew older and infirm. However, his other three sisters were all married successfully. The two youngest, Fanny and Alice, were married at Lugwardine – the former to Robert Thomas Griffiths, a solicitor of Hay-on-Wye, and the latter to Henry Hill, a gentleman from Dymock. His older sister, Ann, eventually married a member of the Hatton family, which had been involved in the tanning business in Hereford for many years.

It was in 1886, at the age of 31, that Alfred married Marion Mendham Cross. She was the daughter of Charles Cross of The Mall, Brentford in Middlesex, in which town the wedding took place. Cross was a wealthy businessman associated with the soap-making firm of Thomas and Berry Rowe, founded in *c*.1787. (The Rowe twins were reputed to be the originals for Dickens' benevolent Cheeryble twins, Charles and Ned, in *Nicholas Nickleby.*) Marion must have found Hereford a great change from Middlesex,

Alfred and Marion's wedding in 1886 (Photographer unknown)

and Alfred a totally different type of person to those with whom she had previously mixed.

In a much later magazine article his daughter, also Marion, was to describe her father as:

a bit of a rough diamond to look at. Broad-shouldered and bearded, he wore (winter and summer) suits of Harris Tweed lined with grey flannel, containing fourteen pockets. These pockets were filled with letters, pamphlets, tools, rulers and other paraphernalia. When the coat was almost too heavy to lift, he would empty the paper content in a heap on a deal table in his 'den'. This room was a scene of apparent chaos, but he could always find everything he wanted.

Perhaps these multitudinous pockets helped him to entertain his children when they were young, for he was considered to be quite a good amateur conjuror.

The newly-weds moved into one of the more pleasant suburbs of Hereford when they rented Sunnyside in Broomy Hill. This is a house of reasonable size in its own grounds and would have been more than satisfactory for the young couple. However, they soon started a family, with Allen, who was born in 1889, and Marion, who was born 17 months later. It was just before Marion was born that the family decided to move to the eastern side of the city where they took over Vineyard Croft in Hampton Park, an impressive, detached, Victorian family house. A two-storey building, the ground floor contained a large reception hall, a drawing room, dining room, study and the usual kitchen and utility rooms. Two staircases led up to the first floor where there were five large bedrooms and a bathroom. The basement contained extensive dry cellarage. The grounds, which contained a substantial coach house, included almost an acre of gardens that continued right down to the banks of the River Wye. It was certainly an ideal place to bring up children and the Watkins stayed there for almost 30 years.

The house, according to Alfred's daughter Marion, was filled with a collection of old English furniture, picked up at moderate prices. The shelves were packed with old and curious books that Alfred fancied. He also collected coarse Staffordshire slip-wares and the pottery designs of the Martin brothers from Southall. Perhaps most evocative were the Arthur Rackham illustrations of Peter Pan which he hung on the walls. The cellars were used for storing fruit and as a dark room for Alfred's photographic work, which became of ever increasing importance during his long stay there.

Vineyard Croft was in a rather odd historical situation, for it was within the parish known as The Vineyard – surely one of the

Alfred Watkins in his late 20s (Bennett & Son, Worcester)

Vineyard Croft from across the River Wye in 1902

Thatching the boathouse at Vineyard Croft

Alfred's wife Marion at Vineyard Croft in about 1891

View across the Wye from Vineyard Croft

smallest parishes in the country, as it had a population of only 13! Alfred was appointed to the honorary position of Overseer for the Poor of this minute parish, a position which could hardly have involved any great effort. The parish, which had originally been a piece of ground belonging to St. Guthlac's Priory, no longer exists as a separate entity.

4

Early writings

Alfred Watkins' first sortie into the field of publication came in 1882 when he supplied the illustrations for a guide book called *Hereford, Herefordshire and the Wye*, written by D.R. Chapman. Mr. Chapman was the librarian and curator of the Hereford Free Library and Museum in Broad Street. This building had been provided by James Rankin, a member of the Woolhope Club, on the understanding that the Woolhopians should have a permanent club room in the building.

It was no doubt due to this generosity that the book, of which five hundred copies were printed for general sale, was dedicated to Rankin, who was then member of parliament for Leominster and chief steward of the city. There were eight illustrations in the book, all taken from photographs by Alfred. He also assisted the author in the compilation of the many walks in the county which are described in the book.

The book is in many ways typical of its period and was designed to cater for the increasing number of people with sufficient leisure time to travel around the countryside and visit the acknowledged beauty spots. However, three copies were very special productions. Each of them contained 33 additional illustrations in permanent platinotype, photographed by Alfred. Hereford is fortunate in possessing one of these copies, which was presented to the city library by the author and photographer on publication. The additional photographs cover a wide variety of subjects and provide a unique picture of life in Herefordshire in the latter part of the 19th century. Many villages and buildings are included, such as the

Cottage at Eardisland

The Toll Gate at Whitney

A Farmyard Scene

The Haymill at Downton

Above, opposite and on the next page: Some of Alfred's early photographs,
included in only three copies of *Hereford, Herefordshire and the Wye* by D.R. Chapman in 1882

market place at Pembridge, street scenes in Ledbury, Eardisland and Weobley, the toll gate at Whitney and the old grammar school at Kington. All Saints Church in Hereford, the old church at Downton and Llanthony Priory show Watkins' interest in religious buildings. However, the photographs which stand out most are the ones depicting countryside events – a Herefordshire hopyard, the haymill at Downton, and two simply labelled as 'a farmyard scene' and 'a cottage scene'.

View of Ross on Wye

The Market Place at Pembridge with the New Inn in the background

The first major piece of research compiled by Alfred alone and marking his debut as an author, was published in *The English Illustrated Magazine*. It was entitled 'A Summer amongst the Dovecots' and included a series of line drawings, by C.M. Gere and E.H. New, of the most important examples, taken from his own photographs. In the article he explains that

> It was with the idea of forming a record of these curious buildings, that I resolved to collect particulars of all in my own county. Many a pleasant tramp, camera on back, through orchard and fallow, along by-roads, over wooded hills, and past thatched cottages, this search entailed.

The article was extended and printed as a booklet in 1891 by William Pollard and Co. of Exeter. This is now very rare as only 75 copies were published – all for private circulation. The booklet was accompanied by an appendix containing a list of all the pigeon houses in Herefordshire visited by the author during 1888 and 1889.

This list of some 74 dovecots includes the type, detailed measurements, the number of nest holes, and, wherever possible, details of dating. Alfred also provided a list of lost pigeon houses, with approximate dates of their demolition. He wrote his article to provide a permanent record of this class of buildings and in doing so he anticipated, by some 90 years, a publication by the county council on the same subject. Further research by Robert Walker recently has resulted in his book *The Dovecots and Pigeon Houses of Herefordshire* (published by Logaston Press in 2010), which includes many of Alfred's photographs. The reasons Alfred gave for his survey are just as valid today, when many redundant barns, small country churches and chapels are being abandoned, often with minimal recording, as dovecots were in the latter part of the 19th century. He said of the dovecots:

> In our county there are still a large number of interesting examples left, but each decade lessens the number, and out of a list of 34 demolished pigeon-houses which I have

Dovecot at Aldersend

Dovecot at Sufton

From the " English Illustrated Magazine," by permission of Messrs. Macmillan & Co.

Drawings of pigeon houses used in Alfred's first major published work. They were taken from original photographs by Alfred as photographic reproduction was still uncommon in the early 1890s.

compiled, not one has, to my knowledge, been described or illustrated. Of the 74 existing examples which I have surveyed (and photographed for the most part) only one, that at Garway, had previously been described. It was this consideration which induced me to make as complete a survey as possible.

The 16-foot-square timber-framed pigeon house at Putson near Hereford, photographed in 1888. (It was demolished in 1889.)

5
The Woolhope Naturalists' Field Club

The Woolhope Club was formed in 1851 for the practical study of the natural history, in all its branches, of Herefordshire and the districts immediately adjacent. It takes its name from the Woolhope Dome, an area to the east of Hereford which is of great interest to geologists. The fine ideals of the original members have continued through to the present day, for the Woolhope Club is still thriving with its members continuing their researches in the fields of archaeology, botany, ornithology and other such subjects.

Alfred Watkins was proposed and elected a member of the club on 24 May 1888, Queen Victoria's 69th birthday. The club was having an outdoor meeting in the Kington area on that day and the formal business, which included his election, was carried out on the summit of Stanner Hill.

The *Transactions* of the club provide many details of the regular meetings held during the latter part of the 19th and the early 20th centuries, and of the research which the members carried out during their field outings. From these we learn that the first meeting Alfred attended was an annual one held in the club room in the City Library.

Once each year the club held a Ladies' Day when the wives and daughters of members were invited to participate in a field trip. Alfred first took his wife, Marion, to one such meeting during June 1889 when the club went to Newland in the Forest of Dean. The secretary recorded this outing as 'one of the happiest days which the annals of the Woolhope Club have been able to place upon record'. The fifty or so members were accommodated in a special railway carriage to Newland. On the outward journey there was a stop at Ross to visit the garden of the president of the club at The Graig, and a second stop at Monmouth for a tour around the town. Then on by train again to Newland, where carriages were in readiness to take the party to the Great Oak Tree near Newland House. The tree was measured, being 43 feet 6 inches around at five feet above the ground – a real monster of an oak!

The carriages then went on to St. Briavels. The weather was good and the roads were dusty – the *Transactions* wryly record 'It was remarkable that more than one lady's hair had turned grey in three-quarters of an hour'. The church and the castle were visited, before the party continued on their journey back towards Monmouth, diverting slightly by Sling's Pit to visit 'one of the "scowles" or "workings of the old men" as the Foresters term them, being traces of Roman workings in their search for iron ore'. On completion of their visit, officials of the Great Western Railway Company ran a special return train from Monmouth at 6.15pm to enable members to catch evening trains home from Hereford.

Alfred went on one more visit the same year, when the club had a joint meeting with the Malvern Field Club, in the Malvern Hills area. There they examined various geological formations, finding several fossils, and then continued to the top of the hills for a walk around the ramparts of the Iron Age hill forts at British Camp and Midsummer Hill.

The annual meeting of the Woolhope Club in April 1890 was the occasion when Alfred read his first paper to the members gathered in the club room. This was entitled *Herefordshire Pigeon-Houses* and the Woolhopians had a rare treat, for Alfred, 'by means of the oxy-hydrogen lantern, reproduced upon the screen a series of photographs, the results of many years' observations'. To produce this effect heavy cylinders of oxygen and hydrogen would have had to be carried up the stairs to the first-floor club room, and the complicated business of persuading the lantern to work efficiently would have taken considerable time. Had this not been enough, he could well have been nervous during his presentation, for one member of the audience was the Reverend Bowell, his headmaster at the Widemarsh Gatehouse School!

It was some time before he went on another expedition with the club, possibly in part due to the births of his two children. But in October 1891 he attended one of their famous 'Fungus Forays'. These were regular yearly events and the early issues of the *Transactions* are well illustrated with colour and black-and-white illustrations of the enthusiasts' findings. The meeting Alfred attended was at Paradise Wood at Pontrilas.

In August 1892 he spent a day with club members on a visit to the Brecon Beacons. The railway from Hereford to Brecon, which had been opened in 1860, was then still thriving (it was to close almost a hundred years after its inception). The directions for organising this type of event and the views to be seen from the train give some indication of the changes in administration of our railways, and the loss we have suffered from the closure of this line and the one which then crossed the Beacons.

Alfred again took his wife to a Ladies' Day meeting in 1893. For this outing the train was taken to New Radnor, and a wagonette was provided, for those who needed it, for the two-and-a-half mile journey to Water-break-its-neck. Ladies' Days were popular and the following year he and his wife went again, this time to Church Stretton for a seven-mile walk to the Long Mynd. It was during 1894 that Alfred Watkins was elected to the central committee of the Woolhope Club.

A different type of meeting was held in June 1896, when 90 members and friends made a first visit to the works of the propri-etors of the Birmingham Water Supply at Elan Valley. This was certainly a meeting that Alfred would not have wanted to miss, for this was the beginning of a very large-scale project which would eventually involve the drowning of several of the mid-Wales valleys. The train was taken to Rhayader, where Mr. Hope-Edwards, of the Royal Inn, provided seats in his carriages for the remainder of the journey 'in a manner creditable to this little town'.

The railway companies continued to be helpful in 1897, when the venue was the Wyre Forest. A special carriage for members of the club was put on the train from Hereford to avoid them having to change at Wooferton Junction on their way to Wyre Forest station.

Alfred decided to take a hand in policy decisions of the club in 1897, when he proposed that each year the *Transactions* should be printed and issued to members at, or immediately after, the end of the year, rather than every two or three years as had been the practice. This motion was not successful – 'the Central Committee decided with regret that they could not see their way to adopt Mr. Watkins' proposition'.

The volume of the *Transactions* for the period 1898-99 was the first to contain many photographs. Presumably the printers, Jakeman and Carver of 4 & 5 High Town, Hereford, had obtained new machinery allowing the economic production of photo-graphic plates. Alfred provided ten photographs for this volume, including a magnificent series showing the work in progress on the Elan dams in 1899. The club had invited members and officials of the Hereford Corporation on this, their second visit to the project. Early starts were the order of the day for Woolhopians – they caught the 7.25am train from Hereford to reach Rhayader at 9.20. From Rhayader the group, numbering over a hundred people, was accommodated in six open trucks with plank seats in which they travelled on the ten miles of the Birmingham Corporation railway, built since their previous visit. They were allowed half-an-hour at each of the four dams, so as not to clash with the regular trains. The whole project had started in 1893 and completion was anticipated in 1902, so the work was more than half finished when this second visit was made.

The middle dam in the Elan Valley scheme during construction in 1899

The 12th-century door-knocker at
Dormington Church

The Woolhope Club at Goodrich Castle (J. Parker, 1917)

Alfred was elected a vice-president of the club for the year 1899, in recognition of his photographic work and of his increasing involvement in the management and organisation of the society. The Woolhope Club did not always meet in distant parts of the county and beyond its borders, and in 1900 there were two local meetings, both attended by Alfred. The first, in June, was to Stoke Edith, Perton and Dormington. Even then the train was used – to Stoke Edith station on the outward journey and Withington station for the return to Hereford. The day included an eight-mile walk as far as the Iron Age camp on Backbury Hill, and dinner, by courtesy of Mr. and Mrs. Scott Hall, under an awning on the lawn of Dormington Court. Alfred must have carried his heavy photo-graphic gear with him, for he photographed Dormington quarry and the fine medieval door-knocker at Dormington Church.

The second meeting was an extra one held in Hereford to visit the cathedral, chained library and Mappa Mundi, and to examine the vestiges of the city walls. Was this when Alfred began to be interested in the evolution of the defences of Hereford, which was eventually to result in several papers for the *Transactions*?

A meeting in 1904 at Lyonshall gave him the chance to read another paper, this time on the subject of Offa's Dyke. The party had taken the train from Hereford to Lyonshall and, after viewing the castle and church, went on to examine the traces of the famous Dyke built by King Offa in the 8th century. From there they went to Almeley for tea and refreshments at the vicarage, and then to Eardisley for dinner at the New Inn. After dinner Alfred read his paper *Offa's Dyke: The Gap in the Weobley District*. He admitted to spending many half-days walking in the area looking for traces of the Dyke between Yazor and Lyonshall. The paper led to a long discussion after which the party, some fifty strong, caught the early evening train from Eardisley station back to Hereford.

Later in 1904 the club visited one of the most inaccessible parts of Herefordshire, where they saw the excavations conducted by C.J. Lilwall at the ruins of the Grandmontine Priory at Craswall. This is one of the most remote of the many monastic sites in the country and one of only three houses of the Grandmontine Order in England. To reach Craswall the party, some 60 strong, walked up from Hay starting at about 10 o'clock in the morning. On their arrival at the priory, Lilwall read a paper on his work, photographs were taken, and the visitors continued to Craswall Church. The walk had covered some eight miles and, although it was then 2.30, the stalwart members 'could not resist the temptation' to ascend Hay Bluff before returning to Hay for a 4.30 luncheon at the Crown Hotel.

Alfred must have found Lilwall's work of great interest, for he took several photographs at the time and accompanied club members on a second visit to examine the extended excavations in 1908, and take further photographs. Because of the remoteness of the site, there had been little stone-robbing since the priory was abandoned in 1442. All that had happened was that the roofs of the main buildings had collapsed and the walls, which survived in places to wall-plate level, were thus buried under the piles of debris. It is unfortunate that the substantial remains cleared by Lilwall were then left open to the elements without any attempt at conservation. In the 80 or so years since Lilwall completed his work the exposed

The chancel at Craswall Priory – the piscina and sedilla on the right. The site had just been excavated when this photograph was taken in 1904.

The remains of a hypocaust excavated at Kenchester in 1912/13. Alfred took most of the photographs of the site during the season's work, including this one.

masonry has suffered considerably. Alfred's photographs were of great help in providing the essential details for the consolidation works which took place in the 1990s.

At the beginning of July 1908 the club visited the Capel-y-Ffin and Llanthony area, where Alfred read a short paper on a dovecot, within the domestic buildings of the priory, that he had discovered during an earlier visit. This was the first time that he was accompanied by his son Allen, then some 19 years old, and though Allen was to accompany his father on several other club expeditions, he never became a member in his own right.

The *Transactions* for the years 1912-13 include an appendix on the excavations by G.H. Jack at the Roman town of Kenchester, some five miles west of Hereford. The preface notes that:

The Kenchester excavations 1912/13

Top: Roman pottery from the excavations
Bottom: One of the mosaic pavements uncovered during the excavations

One feature of the present volume is the vivid excellence of the photographic illustrations, in which details of sculpture etc. can be traced as distinctly as if one stood personally before the objects represented.

With only one exception, all the photographs in both the volume and the appendix were taken by Alfred.

There was only one volume of the *Transactions* issued during the four years of the First World War, but it includes several papers written by Alfred. During these war years he was again elected as vice-president and also became a member of the editorial committee of the club.

Herefordshire Crosses

In successive years, 1916 and 1917, Alfred read two important and related papers to members of the Woolhope Club. The first dealt with Herefordshire Churchyard Crosses, whilst the second considered the position and nature of Herefordshire Wayside and Town Crosses. Each article was profusely illustrated with his own photographs – a record which is now of immense historical and archaeological value, for many of these crosses have disappeared or been damaged in the last 90 years. The survey must have taken much time and effort, for there was no previous complete record and Alfred must have had to visit every town and village in the county and talk to the older villagers to establish the position and history of each cross.

Alfred's interest in crosses may have stemmed from his childhood when he walked the two miles or so out of Hereford on the Hay road to see the remains of the White Cross. This may well have been used as a market cross during the 14th century after the second visitation of the Black Death, and tradition has it that it was erected for that purpose by Bishop Charleton. Alfred recalled making a clay model of it before it was restored in 1867, and made very unfavourable comments about the 'flagstaff-like' shaft added 'out of all proportion' which meant that 'the cross of my childhood seemed spoilt for ever to me'. The restoration work had been supervised by the eminent architect Sir George Gilbert Scott. The several photographs taken

Above: An engraving of the White Cross that Alfred knew and modelled before the 1867 restoration Right: The White Cross after Scott's restoration with the 'flagstaff-like shaft'. Then it stood at the roadside, but when the roads were altered it ended up in the middle of the roundabout.

of this cross by Alfred (one of which is reproduced here) were of considerable help during the recent restoration.

But Alfred was not just interested in recording the details of each cross; he was also concerned about their long term future. Thus, at both Tyberton and Madley, where the churchyard crosses are of considerable interest, a committee of three, composed of Rev. G.W. Turner, Canon Bannister and Alfred himself, was formed to restore the cross-heads.

Most cross-heads had been damaged or completely destroyed during the Reformation and only a few examples survive *in situ* to the present day. The history of the Madley head, as given by Alfred, illustrates the problem of survival and gives an insight into the investigatory research which went in to the production of his article. The cross-head had apparently lain buried in the churchyard for a long time, possibly having been lost at the Reformation. But then it went on a journey:

Top left: The Madley cross with the original head replaced in 1916
Top right: The original head of Tyberton cross was on the chancel gable as shown in this photograph. It was replaced on the original shaft by Woolhope Club members in 1916.
Bottom left: The head of the Tyberton cross with the Virgin and Child.
Bottom right: The opposite side with Christ on the cross.

Many years ago some men working for the late Mr. Edward Bigglestone, a Hereford monumental mason, brought it back from Madley when fixing a headstone there. A Mrs. Lane who lived in Portland Street, begged it from Mr. Bigglestone to ornament her garden. Her brother-in-law, Mr. Tom Maddy, saw it there, and in his turn begged it from Mrs. Lane. Mr. Maddy, who was foreman for our late Assistant Secretary (of the Woolhope Club), Mr. Robert Clarke, gave it to his employer. After Mr. Clarke's death, his widow gave it in charge to the committee to replace it in its right position.

The suggestion which Alfred had made many years previously, that the *Transactions* should be published annually, was finally accepted in 1918 and from then on three annual parts made each complete volume. During the same year the central committee considered the question of ladies becoming members of the club. They decided 'that the indiscriminate admission of ladies would seriously interfere with the scientific objects for which the club was founded'! Apparently this was not entirely to Alfred's satisfaction, for when elected president for the year 1919 he seconded a motion (which was not accepted) that two ladies should be elected as members.

As president of the Woolhope Club Alfred must have felt that he should increase his contributions to the *Transactions*, and in 1919 and 1920 he provided no less than six papers on such diverse subjects as the defences of Hereford, the brooks called Eign, and Garway Church. In the early 1920s, by then in his late 60s, he continued to provide the majority of the photographs used in the *Transactions* and attended most of the club's meetings. The *Transactions* for 1922 has, as a frontispiece, a coloured plate of the early 14th-century stained-glass window at Eaton Bishop Church which had been made from an autochrome photograph taken by him.

In 1917, the club had decided that the *Transactions* should include annual reports from the various Sectional Recorders, and Alfred contributed the section on archaeology from that date until his death – a period of 18 years. These reports are full of interest – prehistoric finds, Roman remains, historic buildings – all indicating his continual observation of the post-

The interior of the church at Clodock with its 17th-century box pews, photographed in 1917, before the church was restored

war regeneration of the county and his contacts with a vast circle of friends. What can often be lost to posterity are details of casual finds such as fleeting glimpses of historic buildings exposed during restorations, coins found during building works, and buried remains unearthed during excavations for new buildings and roads. Alfred, constantly advised by his large collection of friends and acquaintances, made every effort to record and photograph such events, and publish the results. The information, many years later, may give the clue to some otherwise seemingly insignificant event or pattern.

Just a few examples of Alfred's records give some impression of the variety of his observations. In 1917 he noted that Holme Lacy church had its walls underpinned and the floor levels lowered – this could well save future archaeologists much time and effort, for they will know that most archaeological levels will have been either badly disturbed or totally removed. The same issue contains an internal photograph of Clodock Church before the 'ill-kept, dirty, decayed interior of this large mother church' was restored. During the restoration the large box pews were re-ordered to allow for easier access.

In 1921 he recorded Roman finds from the Blackwardine area, a cross-slab found during rebuilding works at the Castle Inn, Ewyas Harold, and Roman remains from Leintwardine. The following year he went out to Peterchurch to record and photograph the 14th-century roof and other features exposed during restoration work at Wellbrook Farm. Typically, he walked around the area and noted a rectilinear earthwork and a mound or tumulus in the orchard at the rear of the house. Two years later he had to record the destruction of the tumulus.

One important publication was *The Old Standing Crosses of Herefordshire*, the result of his many hours of labour in the war years, published in 1930 for the Woolhope Club. In the preface Alfred comments, rather wryly, 'that he had opened more churchyard gates than books during his researches'. Every cross and cross-base is illustrated, many by photographs from his earlier visits, but others taken in 1928 and 1929, when he was in his 70s. The schedule of existing crosses is impressive – a total of 120, all

recorded in considerable detail with exact measurements of all the surviving parts.

He also reported the discovery of several early pottery production sites in Herefordshire – in effect an appendix to a series of articles he had written and illustrated on the subject which went back as far as 1917. Knowledge of early pottery kilns is of great significance to modern archaeologists interested in the methods of production and the distances that the wares would have travelled from their sources to the final points of use. From this type of information a picture of late medieval and earlier trading patterns is now beginning to emerge. The first essential is to have available the earlier records of the sources of the individual wares, and Alfred's records provide this information for Herefordshire and the surrounding areas.

The various potteries noted by him include one discovered in 1916 by the son of the stationmaster at Whitney in the aptly named Kiln Ground Wood which was 'being cut down by Finns employed by the government and encamped here'. Many examples of this well-made and well-distributed 17th-century pottery are described.

Pottery fragments recovered from Birtley, Lingen, photographed in 1931

It took several visits to Grove Head at Lingen before Alfred and several of his friends found the spoil heaps which were associated with this pottery production site on the banks of the Lime Brook within the ancient Deerfold Forest. Samples of this early 17th-century ware were collected and are illustrated in photo-

graphs. Another of these 17th-century 'cottage industries' was discovered near Kempley in 1928.

The Woolhope Club's well-planned visits by train gradually came to an end with the advent of the motor car and the charabanc which was increasingly used after the war. Thus, on the

Caradoc Court at Sellack in 1928, since gutted by fire, but now fully restored. This picture shows the timber framework on the riverside elevation.

Ladies' Day visit to Eardisley, Clifford and Bredwardine in 1928, they drove much of the way, only walking from Middlewood over Merbach (for the magnificent views) and then via Arthur's Stone down to Bredwardine. The following meeting, in southern Herefordshire, included a visit to Caradoc Court, where the visitors were entertained to tea. Alfred took several photographs of the 15th-century timber-framed parts of the building which were used as an aid to reconstruction work following the disastrous fire in 1986.

The vexed question of the admission of ladies to the club was again discussed at a special general meeting in 1931. Alfred spoke at length in favour of their admission and was reported as saying that:

> He remembered the time when almost everyone who joined the club used a microscope and was seriously interested in photography. Today the craft of photography was dead ... the study of botany and of mycology was also almost dead. There had, however, been a tremendous change in another direction – women were waking up and taking an interest in the things which men had dropped.

His suggestion that the club was a dying society was received with loud cries of dissent and, despite his impassioned plea, the motion to admit ladies was lost by 46 votes to 11. Ladies were not to be admitted as full members until after his death.

He continued to present information to the club almost until the end of his life. He read a most useful paper to members in December 1931 which was based on his memories of Hereford going back over 70 years. *Hereford Place-names and Sites* provides modern-day archaeologists and historians with an important reference list of streets, ancient sites, official buildings, cross-sites, gates and toll-gates, wharves, prisons, burial-grounds, wells, etc. within the city.

His last two papers both concerned aspects of the city. *Foundations of Buildings in Hereford Castle* recorded his observa-tions of parch marks on Castle Green. The paper was prompted by:

> the long drought of 1933, when the sun of our glorious summer had bleached in patches the turf on the Castle Green, as if on a stony hillside, leaving parch marks between the green of normal pasture. In places, straight lines of whitened grass of even width appeared, with other lines at right angles, forming in at least three cases (which I roughly surveyed and measured up) the outlines of foundations of rectilinear buildings, twenty to twenty-seven feet in length, and with walls two to four feet thick. Beside these were two long lines of similar marks, probably boundary walls, although a suggestion has been made that they mark the line of underground passages.

Alfred considered one of the buildings to be a tower and the other a chapel, but was never to see his theories proved. However, in 1960, small trial excavations by F.G. Heys on the latter site confirmed the accuracy of the 27-year-old theory, exposing parts

Parch marks on Castle Green, indicating the buried foundations of long-lost buildings, photographed in 1933

The Freemen's Prison which adjoined the Booth Hall in Hereford, shortly before it was demolished. Taken in 1934, this may have been the last photograph taken by Alfred.

of the nave and chancel. The traces of buried foundations can still be seen, as long parch marks in the grass, whenever there is a dry summer. They relate to some of the many buildings which once stood on Castle Green and which, according to an inventory of 1265, included three halls: the king's great hall, the king's small hall, and the county hall.

Alfred's final paper was entitled *The Freemen's Prison at the Boothall* where he recorded the architectural details and historical connections of yet another historic building in the city before it was demolished.

Even in his late 70s, Alfred was still out and about in the country areas taking photographs of longstones, cup-marked stones and stone mortars. The 1933 Woolhope Club Archaeology Report includes no less than 23 of his photographs taken in many parts of the county.

6
Ley Lines

When Alfred Watkins read a paper to members of the Woolhope Club in September 1921 he could not possibly have had any idea of the repercussions it would have throughout the whole world.

His subject was innocuous enough – at least as far as the title of the talk was concerned. 'Early British Trackways, Moats, Mounds, Camps and Sites' could well have been taken to be intended as a wide-ranging talk on archaeological features throughout the countryside – a subject on which the speaker was well qualified. But this was most certainly not Alfred's intention. Instead he made use of the lecture to introduce to his fellow members a totally new concept – that of 'the old straight track'.

The *Transactions* of the Woolhope Club do not give any indication of what the members present thought of this radical idea from one of their most respected members. At the close of the meeting the president of the day merely said that the speaker 'had shown them how they could use their eyes, and he hoped they would study the subject upon which, in so illuminating a manner, Mr. Watkins had spoken'.

It was on 30 June 1921, when Alfred was on a chance visit to a part of the Herefordshire countryside he knew very well, that the whole idea 'came to me in a flash'. He explained to the meeting:

> A visit to Blackwardine led me to note on the map a straight line starting from Croft Ambrey, lying on part of Croft Lane past the Broad [a hamlet between Leominster and Luston], over hill points, through Blackwardine, over Risbury Camp, and through the high ground at Stretton Grandison, where I surmise a Roman station. I followed up the clues of sight from hill top, unhampered by other theories, found it yielding astounding results in all districts, the straight lines to my amazement passing over and over again through the same class of objects, which I soon found to have been practical sighting points.

He was later to describe his concept as follows:

> Imagine a fairy chain stretched from mountain peak to mountain peak, so far as the eye could reach, and laid out until it touched the high places of the earth at a number of ridges, banks and knowls. Then visualise a mound, circular earthwork, or clump of trees, planted on these high points, and in low points in the valley, other mounds ringed round with water to be seen from a distance. Then great standing stones brought to mark the way at intervals, and on a bank leading up to a mountain ridge or down to a ford the track cut deep so as to form a guiding notch on the skyline as you come up. In a bwlch or mountain pass the road cut deeply to show as a notch afar off. Here and there, and at two ends of the way, a beacon fire used to lay out the track. With ponds dug on the line or streams banked up into 'flashes' to form reflecting points on the beacon track so that it might be checked when at least once a year the beacon was fired on the traditional day. All these works exactly on the sighting line.

In essence what Alfred was suggesting was that during the whole of the prehistoric period all trackways used by traders and others followed straight lines marked out on a sighting system from hill to hill and using mark points in between. He insisted that this was demonstrated by the alignment, across miles of countryside, of a great number of objects, or sites of objects, of prehistoric antiquity – not just in a few examples but in hundreds of cases. He was to spend much of the rest of his life in accumulating evidence to demonstrate his idea and in publishing the results of his researches.

The sighting line (or ley, as it became known because of the number of places on the alignment with 'ley' in the name) needed regular marking or sighting points which could easily be seen by the user standing at the preceding point. These secondary points were the basis of Alfred's discovery, for many were objects which were marked on maps and he considered them to be acceptable if straight lines could be drawn joining four or more ancient sites. The sighting points were constructed of earth, water or stone, although trees could also have been planted on the line. The lines could be drawn through a variety of points, for the original markers, being important objects in the landscape, had subsequently been re-used and their sites marked by later, but still historic, features.

Earth sighting points included all the various types of mounds – tumuli, barrows, cairns, castle mottes, etc. – and also notches in banks or mountain ridges. Water sighting points, usually on low ground, such as moats and artificial ponds, formed a point or ring of reflection from higher ground. Mark stones were stones of various shapes and sizes, deliberately placed by the side of the track.

Iron Age camps, or hill forts as they are now usually known, often appeared on maps to be the focus of several leys which were usually aligned with the higher parts of the earthworks rather than their centre. Thus Alfred was to note

Title page from *Early British Trackways*, published in 1922

Plate from *Early British Trackways*, published in 1922. The caption read:
Leys Displayed: 1. Track Climbing Ridge, Llanthony Abbey
2. Straight Wye-side Causeway, Bartonsham, Hereford

with Capler Camp that it had 'so many leys over it as to seem to be the Clapham Junction of ancient trackways in that district'.

Churches or churchyard crosses, if ancient, were almost invariably to be found on one or more leys and Alfred suggested that the church or cross replaced an earlier mark stone, and pointed out the frequent coincidence of mounds or moats with early church sites. Castles, particularly those comprising a motte, also appeared on several leys, and he assumed that an earlier sighting mound had been re-used as the site for a castle. It followed from the argument that 'the old straight track' decided, in the long-lost past, the site of almost every branch of human communal activity. Thus churches were often built at the crossing of two leys whilst homesteads, and eventually villages, were associated with earlier ponds or moats used as sighting points.

As a result of his researches, Alfred was convinced that the frequency of ley lines, passing through historic sites used as mark points, was much too common to be due solely to coincidence; his theory was based not just on dim folk memories, but on a carefully accumulated collection of data. Collecting such evidence enabled him to expand on his lecture to the Woolhope Club in a book entitled *Early British Trackways*, published in 1922, less than a year after his original discovery. He later described the book as a 'somewhat breathless production' which was sent to press only five months after he had the first clue, but it still provides the clearest exposition of his theory as it applied to Herefordshire. Apart from being the first publication on the subject of ley lines, the book has one other claim to fame – it was bound by a man called Buckridge who was later to be convicted of the murder of his wife and her foster-mother!

Ignoring the indexes, the many photographs and the two maps, there are 27 pages of text. These range from a clear introduction to the subject as a whole, a definition of ley lines and the different types of sighting points (all with many examples), evidence from place-names, to hints to ley hunters, and a list of several leys.

Alfred expounded on his ley line theory at every available opportunity. Thus, at a Ladies' Day meeting of the Woolhope Club in 1922 at Courtfield, he described two leys which went through the mound adjacent to the mansion. He followed this with a paper in 1924 in which he described an alignment running from Giant's Cave, on the Eastnor side of the Malvern Hills, through a stone known as the Sacrificial Stone, thence via the churches at Woolhope and Holme Lacy, to a pond on top of the Deer Park, and then through Aconbury Church to finish at the highest point on Aconbury Camp. Not content with this remarkable alignment through no less than seven points, he also noted that both Woolhope and Holme Lacy churches were on the same exact alignment as the ley. In addition, the sun, rising above the ridge of the cave at six o'clock on Midsummer's Day, falls directly on the Sacrificial Stone and thus on the ley. One can well understand his wry comment: 'This can scarcely be a coincidence'.

The 'sacrificial stone' near to the Giant's Cave on the Malvern Hills in 1924. Alfred evidently had a willing volunteer for his photograph!

Plate from *Early British Trackways*. The caption read:
Markstones: Top left, Red Lion Madley; Top right Credenhill;
Bottom left, Wye Street, Hereford; Bottom right, Bartonsham

One of the most extraordinary standing stones in Herefordshire is the Queen Stone at Huntsham. It stands in the middle of a meadow within the horseshoe bend of the River Wye which also includes Symond's Yat. When Alfred first knew it, the stone stood some 2.3m high above ground level (ploughing has since reduced the amount visible a little) with the main face 1.6m wide and the thickness 1.1m. All the sides contain deep vertical grooves, 5 to 6cm wide and up to 18cm deep.

Alfred had established from maps that the Queen Stone was a mark stone on at least three separate alignments and, because of its unusual design and position, he decided to organise an excavation around the base of the stone. This took place in September 1926, and to his surprise he found that the deep grooves all stopped abruptly at the then ground level, although about 2.4m of the stone was buried under the ground. He established from his excavations that the original hole for the stone had been dug with one straight and one sloping side and suggested that the stone had been slid in and raised against the vertical face, the base on the other side being then packed with stones before the hole was filled. Within the excavations were several worked flints, fragments of burnt bone and large quantities of charcoal.

From the design of the stone and the objects found in association with it, Alfred deduced that, apart from its use as a ley marker, it had also been used as a sacrificial stone. He suggested that long osier rods could have been placed in each groove to form a rough 'cage' or 'basket' above the stone, the whole being bound with withies. The sacrificial object would then have been put within the cage and the whole was then fired. He provides, in his article on the subject in the Woolhope Club *Transactions*, an account of a similar practice which was apparently carried out by the Druids and described in Caesar's *War in Gaul*.

Some seven years later, when he was 78 years old, Alfred volunteered to give a talk on the subject to some 500 Woodcraft Folk who were camped around the Queen Stone. This organised camp movement drew its members from the co-operative and kindred bodies, typically from the larger cities. In preparation for this talk, the

The Queen Stone at Huntsham with its peculiar vertical grooves. This photograph was taken during the excavations arranged by Alfred in 1924 and shows the length of the stone that was buried.

Woodcraft Folk built a 'cage' on the stone to Alfred's specifications, complete with two 'victims' inside. The event was captured on film – the only known cinematographic representation of Alfred Watkins.

He followed his paper on the Queen Stone with one in 1927 on the Wergins Stone, which stands in a field some four miles north of Hereford near Sutton. This 1.5m high stone, with its roughly pentagonal base, he also considered to be a mark stone. In addition, the stone has had rather an odd reputation, gaining the alternative name of the Devil's Stone, for in the 1695 edition of Camden's *Britannica* it appears in an account of what would seem to be a rather purposeless miracle.

> Between Sutton and Hereford, in a common meadow called the Wergins, were placed two large stones for a water mark, one erected upright, the other laid athwart. In the late civil wars, about the year 1652, they were removed to about twelve score paces distance, and nobody knows how; which gave occasion to a common opinion that they were carried thither by the Devil. When they were set in their places again, one of them required nine yoke of oxen to draw it.

A year later Alfred, still continuing his researches into mark points, read a paper to the Woolhope Club on Arthur's Stone, the well-known megalithic burial chamber on top of Merbach Hill, above the village of Bredwardine in west Herefordshire. He describes it in some detail and refers to earlier records of a ring of stones around the monument and also of excavations on the site. He then describes the various alignments he had discovered which went through the mound which had originally covered the stone burial chamber.

In 1925 Alfred completed what was to be his most famous book – *The Old Straight Track* – which has been regularly reprinted to the present day. From the preface to the original edition the reader can get some idea of the way that Alfred saw his great idea when he commented that 'in fully half a century's familiar contact with this region my other self had, quite unknown to me, worked at one subject'. The book was the result of almost four years' strenuous fieldwork, all carried out during his late 60s, to provide what he considered to be the necessary evidence to prove his case.

The contents of *The Old Straight Track* follow a similar order to those in his previous book *Early British Trackways*, but with far

Alfred giving a talk to the Woodcraft Folk in 1933 watched by two 'victims' in a wicker cage built above the Queen Stone
(Photographer unknown)

Arthur's Stone, a megalithic burial chamber on Merbach Hill above Bredwardine. Alfred established four alignments which he considered to go through the site.

more details on the various types of sighting points – mounds, moats, mark stones etc. – and including beacons for the first time. In chapter eleven he discusses the skilled men who originally laid out the ley lines. He based much of his evidence for these people on place names and from his studies came to the conclusion that it was the 'cole-man' who gave his name to many points and places on the tracks, and that he must have been the head-man of the team who made them. This followed from the many place names incorporating 'cole' which he found were associated with leys over the country as a whole. The surveyor was the 'dod-man' who used two long sighting staves. He considered that this ancient surveyor was commemorated in the Long Man of Wilmington, the 240 feet long prehistoric figure, complete with two staves, cut into the turf on the hillside at Wilmington in Sussex. Finally the tenderer of the beacon, an essential part of the construction team for these were usually at the beginning of leys, was the 'black-man'.

Examples in other lands, biblical references to the straight track, confirmation of leys in other parts of the British Isles, and a discussion of objections to the theory, all make the book compulsive reading. It also contains well over a hundred photographic illustrations by the author (mainly taken in Herefordshire and the surrounding area). The book was the culmination of over half-a-century's familiarity with the region he loved so well. When it was first published the reviewer in the *New Statesman* said:

> Only an out-of-doors man could have written this book, and only a man with a student's critical faculty could have weighed and dovetailed the evidence here collected. It is admirably illustrated and a first-rate piece of work.

On the whole Alfred's discovery was ignored by contemporary academic archaeologists, who would not even consider the existence of ley lines and mark points and for many years were not prepared to discuss the subject. *The Old Straight Track* was considered to be so radical that the editor of the archaeological journal *Antiquity* refused to include a paid advertisement, let alone review it.

In 1926 Alfred helped in the formation of 'The Straight Track Club', a loose organisation of interested amateurs who circulated news of their discoveries through a series of postal portfolios. The club held a three days' meeting in Hereford in 1933 when Alfred was president and he arranged a joint meeting with the Woolhope Club where he spoke on *A Sacrificial Stone at Lydney*. It was probably the formation of this club that encouraged Alfred to write *The Ley Hunter's Manual*, a practical guide to early tracks, published in 1927. This 90-page book, with some 64 illustrations, was well received as can be seen from the review in the *Birmingham Gazette* which noted:

> It is given to few people to create, even on a small scale, a new out-door hobby. That is what Mr. Watkins did by his field work and writing on leys or early British trackways.

Some reviewers were not so kind and one, after reading *Archaic Tracks Round Cambridge*, tried a practical experiment:

> Reflecting on the instinct of the unregenerate walker to make for the nearest pub, the reviewer took the same one-inch map and selecting inns as his sight-marks, obtained similar results to Mr. Watkins. His first, and best, effort produced six inns in line; another, four inns and the significant place name Two Pots House. Four lines of four inns can be drawn, each terminating on one of the Noon Follies [associated with Watkins' midday sighting lines]; and considering the original meaning of noon – about 3 o'clock – and the impossibility of obtaining a drink at that hour, the result is no doubt significant and our English road system is to be attributed to Mr. Watkins' sight-walker, gradually developing into Mr. Chesterton's reeling English drunkard.

Such criticism did not unduly worry Alfred and indeed he continued to emphasise that ley hunting gave a new zest to field rambles. In *Early British Trackways* he had a mental vision of a scoutmaster of the future instructing his troops – 'Now we have found the ley, I think we shall see a bit of the old track in that far grassy field this side the moat; it's narrow and straight, and there are many who never find it because they look for a broad way like our present wheel tracks'.

Archaic Tracks Round Cambridge, published in 1932, is Alfred's only book that detailed ley lines in an area outside his home county. He admits in his introduction that the book is only a framework for local and field investigation for the two branches of enquiry – map and field work. In the book he offers the former but leaves the field work 'to those who, by health-giving tramps along the lines indicated, will, I feel sure, find new corroboration'. He indicates that the work was a result of a flying visit to Cambridge during which a glance at local maps had indicated that the district was remarkably rich in mark-point evidence. He was visiting his son, Allen, who worked in Cambridge at that time. Allen, a fervent believer in ley lines, said of the book that it had many claims to be considered the best his father ever wrote, even though he only took a couple of months in both the research and the writing.

He starts the book, as he did the two earlier ones, with a description of his discovery, and then uses this as a basis for the investigation which follows. He goes on to discuss the arguments against accidental coincidence which several critics had raised. In the third chapter he describes seven alignments through the borough of Cambridge. This is expanded in chapter four where he includes a reduced version of the one-inch popular edition of the Ordnance Survey map showing a multiplicity of straight alignments all within an area of some 12 miles around Cambridge. In all, 25 alignments are shown and described, each with a minimum

of five mark points. He goes on to consider the origin of the most famous of the older roads in the Cambridge area – Ermine Street, Icknield Way, Akeman Street and Via Devana – and presents mark-point evidence for what he sees as their original courses before they became the straight roads that are known today.

He then discusses the possibility that some of the alignments are seasonal (e.g. associated with the midsummer sunrise), that some churches are aligned on leys constructed from earlier sighting marks, and that several of the leys around Cambridge are aligned with the cardinal points of the compass. He compares the evidence for the latter theory with the cardinal point alignments he had discovered in the Radnor Forest area where they were apparently associated with cup-marked stones.

In the final chapter he mentions Dr. Cyril Fox's scholarly work *The Archaeology of the Cambridge Region*, which he had read on completion of his own work. He comments that the author:

> naturally adopts the orthodox opinion (I think, wrongly), that straightness and alignment is an exclusive sign of Roman engineering, all earlier ones being sinuous. This excepted I find his attitude and information as to prehistoric tracks and their mark-points amazingly full, up-to-date, and open-minded.

He concludes his own book by apologising for the lack of photographs, which he blames on his advancing years, and hopes that others will follow up with the field work pointing out that 'adventure lies lurking in these lines where I point the way for younger feet than mine'.

Public life and personal enthusiasms

It is fortunate that Allen Watkins, Alfred's son, was sufficiently impressed by his father and his life that he decided to write 'a first-hand account … [of] his life and pioneer work in the three worlds of archaeology, photography and flour milling'. *Alfred Watkins of Hereford* was published in a 'signed limited edition only' in 1972. In addition, his daughter, Marion, wrote an article in two parts for *The Lady* – 'Victorian Portraits; some family reminiscences'. In the first part she describes her grandfather's life and family, and in the second part deals with her home life as she grew up in Hereford. From these sources a gradual picture of Alfred emerges:

> His contacts with rural society were many – with farmers at the Corn Exchange, with country bakers, with parsons and farm labourers. His sympathies were very much with the latter, who at that time earned between 11s. and 13s. a week, on which they had to keep a family.
>
> Politics were a very live issue in the city at that time and Alfred Watkins was one of the stalwarts of the Liberal Party. His was the traditional liberalism of Milton, Morley, Mill, Gladstone, and Asquith; an idealist force which largely moulded nineteenth-century England. … My Father's Liberalism was almost a religion with him and coloured his whole outlook. He considered that the farm worker was the salt of the earth; the true aristocrat of the land; and had had a raw deal throughout history. …
>
> He favoured a wide franchise, to include women, and, like many Liberals, regarded the vote as a sacred privilege.

He wanted justice for all, but disliked socialism. To him justice meant a fair chance; not an equal share of wealth.

> He preferred private enterprise to collective ownership for the simple reason that with the former the burden of any loss fell on the responsible agent and ended there, but in the latter, on the innocent public. That is a piece of Alfred Watkins logic worth remembering in the present days of mounting prices.
>
> He had a strong sense of public duty himself, and thought everyone ought to have it too. If *noblesse* failed to *oblige*, it was contemptible. He despised private selfishness.

In 1905/6 he organised and spoke at small lantern-lecture meetings all over the county in favour of Free Trade and against Joseph Chamberlain's proposal for protective tariffs. Allen Watkins commented:

> I have a vivid recollection of those meetings. One old farm labourer remembered the Corn Laws and the Hungry Forties. I was seeing English history at first hand – in 1840 as it was in the raw. These meetings were well attended by the village audiences and had a considerable political effect.

One of Alfred's early successes in the realm of public life was in 1893, when he was 'the leader in a citizens' agitation' to construct the footpath that now runs from the Victoria Suspension Bridge downstream, underneath what was the wall of the General Hospital

Top left: In 1896 Alfred took this picture of the
Wye below the General Hospital grounds, where
he had helped organise a new path and garden.
The makeshift summer 'bridge' was replaced by the
suspension bridge in 1898.
Bottom left: A fête in aid of the Herefordshire
Volunteers held in the grounds
of Vineyard Croft in 1915
Above: The War Memorial in St. Peter's Square,
Hereford. Alfred chaired the committee which
selected this Eleanor Cross design.
(Ken Hoverd, 1990)

grounds together with the little garden adjoining it. Perhaps this should now be called Watkins Walk, after the ill-fated attempt some years ago by the then City Council to commemorate him by naming the passage leading from Widemarsh Street to the Tesco car park through the Mansion House as Watkins Passage. Although the sign was put up, it rapidly disappeared after complaints from his daughter that he deserved much better!

In 1914 he was selected to be the Military Representative on the Hereford Recruiting Tribunal – the local organisation which decided whether people applying for postponement of conscription on either business or personal grounds had a legitimate case. During the First World War, he organised almost a hundred recruiting meetings, and he and Ann hosted fund-raising events at Vineyard Croft. In 1915 he became County Councillor for the Tupsley division. By this time his children had grown up and he had ceased to be involved, on a day-by-day basis, with the family's various business enterprises. He continued to represent the Tupsley division until he became an Alderman in 1934.

In spite of his extensive private researches, he continued to do a great deal of public work. He served on the Bench of Magistrates, and as Governor of the local High Schools, and Chairman of the School of Arts and Crafts Committee. He was probably the longest-serving member of the Library Committee of the City Council, serving from 1880 to 1934, and he also sat on the Education and Old House Committees, and on the Board of Directors of the Green Dragon Hotel, Hereford. His daughter commented that: 'He was a frequent speaker at every contest on behalf of Free Trade or any other issue. What fun the city worthies had keeping their hand in at the Town Hall in a mock parliament!'

The executive committee responsible for the county and city War Memorial in St. Peter's Square held all their deliberations under Alfred's chairmanship, and he must have had considerable influence on their choice of the design of the Eleanor Cross.

In 1902 he was appointed as a trustee of the Hereford Municipal Charities and rendered much valuable service to this body for over thirty years.

Alfred's daughter Marion tree-felling in around 1915, as part of the war effort

Bees and Bee-keeping

In 1882 Alfred was a member of the founding committee of the Herefordshire Bee-keepers Association and was its secretary until 1901. Towards the end of the 19th century the association, with help from the County Council, took on a public role by attempting to popularise and teach good and efficient bee-keeping. This was achieved by means of a horse-drawn bee van which toured the Herefordshire countryside, the instructor giving practical demonstrations in some bee-keeper's garden. And then 'as shades of night began to fall the pictures ... are shown on a screen filling up the end of the van'. For this purpose, Alfred had prepared a series of lantern slides on the subject. Eventually the slides were accompanied with a booklet that he wrote – *Bees and Bee-keeping* – for a series called *Optical Lantern Readings*. The booklet lists and describes some 30 slides including some which, at that time, would have been difficult to photograph.

The Bee Van attracting a rather sceptical-looking audience

They included 'the abdomen of the worker bee' and 'the antenna comb on the first leg', both of which must have been taken using a microscope.

In 1919, following his presidential year at the Woolhope Club, Alfred decided that, rather than offer an archaeological subject, he would take as a topic 'the one natural-history subject on which I am sufficiently qualified to speak, that of the only insect which we in the British Isles subserve to the use of man – the honey-bee'. He described, with slides, the history of the honey bee and its importance after the Norman Conquest when the Domesday Survey records Welsh tenants in Archenfield as paying their dues in honey. He went on to describe the methods of early bee-keeping, the various aspects of hives, how to retain swarms, and aspects of the law relating to bees.

One of Alfred's series of photographs on bee-keeping. The fine frame hives in the picture indicate a great improvement from the older straw bee skeps that resulted in the death of the bees when the honey was taken. Here the honey is being taken from the frame.

Alfred Watkins gathering a swarm of bees

Tenths or Octets?

Alfred's fertile mind took him into what might today be considered as a strange avenue. One of his most unusual published works, issued through the Watkins Meter company, should perhaps have been reprinted in the 1960s. *Must We Trade In Tenths?* was published in 1919 just after the end of the Great War. Alfred described it as 'a plea against decimal and for octaval coinage as more exactly fitting the wants and usage of all who make, grow, buy or sell things'. At this time there were proposals for a decimal currency based on 1,000 mils to £1 (inflation 50 years later made this 100 pence to £1!) Alfred went into considerable detail to demonstrate that his ideas were superior to those being proposed. His basic philosophy was that for trading purposes it would be much more convenient if currency, weights and measures were based on the series 2, 4, 8, 16, 32 etc, and the corresponding fractions of half, quarter, eighth and so on, allowing divisions up and down to the unit 1. The fatal defect of the decimal system, as Alfred saw it, was that 10 only halves to five – a prime number.

For those who have forgotten, the pre-decimal currency consisted of 12 pence to a shilling and 20 shillings to the pound. The coins above the shilling were the florin (two shillings or one-tenth of a pound; first issued in 1849 so that people might 'get educated to decimals') and the half-crown (two shillings and six pence). The basis of Alfred's proposed currency was: the pound split into eight half-crowns; the half-crown split into 8 groats; and the groat split into eight cents. The coinage would have been in multiples of 4, 2, and 1 of each unit below the pound, each coin being half the value of the previous in an unbroken series down to its 512th part – the cent. Calculations would have been interesting, to say the least – for the digits 8 and 9 would not have been used in this currency. He continued his battle against the proposed decimal currency in a letter to *The Nation* (a liberal journal), where he was supported by no less a figure than George Bernard Shaw.

The Final Years

It was in 1919, after their two children had left home, that the Watkins moved to a smaller house in Harley Court, the narrow passage linking the Cathedral Close to the rear of the Town Hall. In September 1919 they invited members of the Woolhope Club to hear Alfred give a talk on *Three Timber-framed Halls in the City of Hereford* – the Bishop's Palace; the Booth Hall (recently opened up and conserved) and the building in which the meeting was held i.e. 5 Harley Court. The timber roof of the hall at that time was completely hidden by a false ceiling, but Alfred had obtained a drawing made by W.W. Robinson, who had superintended works to the building in 1884. The false ceiling has since been removed to expose the finely decorated roof timbers of a 15th-century hall that was once the home of one of the canons of the cathedral.

His son, Allen, eventually married and in 1920 a grandson, Felix, was born. Many years later, Felix remembered 'kissing a rather prickly gentleman, who was clearly glad to see me, but who almost at once disappeared into his sanctum at the top of the stairs'. From time to time he went out with his grandfather in his car – then a Jowett, for steam cars, Alfred's favourites, were no longer available (he had previously had a Gardner-Serpollet, a Stanley and a Pearson-Cox; all steam cars) – stopping at historic sites and archaeological excavations.

Family memories often give an indication of the personality of their parents, and Allen recollected a poem his father often recited:

Bloaters and bats for breakfast,
Sparrows and sprats for tea,
New milk in vats
For respectable cats,
Industrious cats like me.

Rabbits and rats for dinner
Mice and their brats for tea,
Best butter pats
For respectable cats,
Industrious cats like me.

Harley Court from the Town Hall window, taken in 1922

5 Harley Court, the Watkins' home from 1919 to 1935

Alfred was a great believer in steam cars and lorries. Here he is seen in his Gardner-Serpollet car in 1908. These cars were produced in France at the beginning of the 20th century. The oil-fired flash boiler fed steam to a very advanced four-cylinder enclosed engine similar to the contemporary petrol engine design.

The last 15 years of Alfred's life were fully occupied with his theories on ley-lines, with his continuing stream of publications, with the affairs of the Woolhope Club and the Herefordshire Photographic Society, and with the affairs of the city and county that he knew and loved so well.

Alfred had little thought for his own health and tended to neglect an internal problem. His son commented that:

> During the nine months of illness that preceded his death, he began to have some out-of-the-way experiences. He told me that when he turned on the wireless he often heard the exact words of the announcer before they were spoken. He once proved this capacity by writing in a sealed envelope. ... He said to me 'I have been psychic all my life, but I have kept it under wraps and never told anyone about it'. Serious reflection on these manifestations of unseen intelligence had convinced father for some time that in reality the human soul is independent of its material trappings. He was a firm believer, but had no time for ecclesiasticism.

After some nine months of illness, Alfred died at his home on 7 April 1935. The funeral service took place in the cathedral's Lady Chapel, which was full to capacity. There were press comments nationwide, and the *Daily Express* paid tribute in a leading article:

A fancy dress ball at the School of Art in about 1930. Alfred was Chairman of Governors and took part in events (he can be seen on the right).
The young girl in the front was eventually to marry Alfred's grandson.

JUST CITIZEN

A good citizen died yesterday, the kind which keeps the public life of the countryside on the highest plane of any in the world.

His name was Alfred Watkins. You can conjure with it in Herefordshire and the counties of the Welsh border. He was scholar, miller, farmer, archaeologist, naturalist, inventor, magistrate, county councillor, politician, and leader of public opinion. He was full of years and honours.

You could say of him what Earl of Morton said at the graveside of John Knox: 'Here lies one who never feared nor flattered any flesh'.

His obituary filled two columns of the *Hereford Times*. The writer, a friend for some twenty years, asked:

Who in the city can be unfamiliar with that slightly bent figure intense, abrupt, hurrying to some business or engaged in animated conversation, oblivious to anything save the object in hand? ... Under his brusque manner lay a nature kindly, generous and just. All will miss him, and with his passing goes a landmark in Hereford life and history. All his life was spent here; rarely leaving it even for holidays, he loved the villages, lanes, churches, hills and mounds, explored and photographed the county from end to end, and had an intimate knowledge of its physical details which few others can have achieved without such a lifetime affection.

First and foremost he was a Herefordshire man, as native to the county as the hop and the apple.

The Masefield Country

by

Alfred Watkins

This rustic cottage at Bridge Sollers might have been one built in the gardens of The Weir, where one was recorded by James Wathen in 1799.

Preface

On the eastern edge of that lovely and – as yet – unspoilt English county, of which the old city of Hereford is the centre, one is especially favoured with a crumpled region of wooded hills. Here, within a couple of miles, three poets – William Langland, Elizabeth Barrett and John Masefield – were reared, and the close links between their life-work and the beauty of their own particular bit of motherland is the motive for this book.

How often the character of a living person has been partly moulded by the influence of his native countryside. John Masefield, in his moving poem *August 1914*, has shown the countryman torn between the conflicting claims of the country as a whole, and his clinging to 'the heartfelt things' of his loved countryside; and how, after 'brooding by the fire with heavy mind' the call for king and country prevailed. An experience gained in a hundred recruiting meetings in the voluntary phase of Kitchener's call for 'more and more men' and at a tribunal in the later, compulsory stage, showed me that different types of countryside, even in this one shire, bred differences of attitude to the call. In the mountainside places where farms held rights of grazing on the hills, the call of home soil often obliterated that of national need, and few responded in such hill-land. Can we doubt that the beauty of this west-country homeland has done much to create and foster the poetic genius of these three writers, born in different ages?

The inspiration to write this book came in a day – that memorable day when we heard the Poet Laureate let fall on us what our young member for South Herefordshire [Frank Owen] has since designated 'the most beautiful speech that any of us will probably ever hear in our lives'. Next day I began to write this book.

I soon found that I had really been collecting for these pages through the 57 years of my adult life, during which both my occupations and the call of open air had brought ample opportunities to store up, a bit at a time, partly through camera lens, and partly by observation and pen-note, fragments of material evidence of the link which is now my subject matter.

I therefore try to rake together the modest harvest which in a year or two would have been lost. The record cannot be impersonal, for into it has to be woven certain threads of my own life, necessary to the presentation of evidence. This is the reason for more use of the first person singular than would be otherwise desirable.

Alfred Watkins

Hereford, May 1931

Map indicating many of the places mentioned in *The Masefield Country*

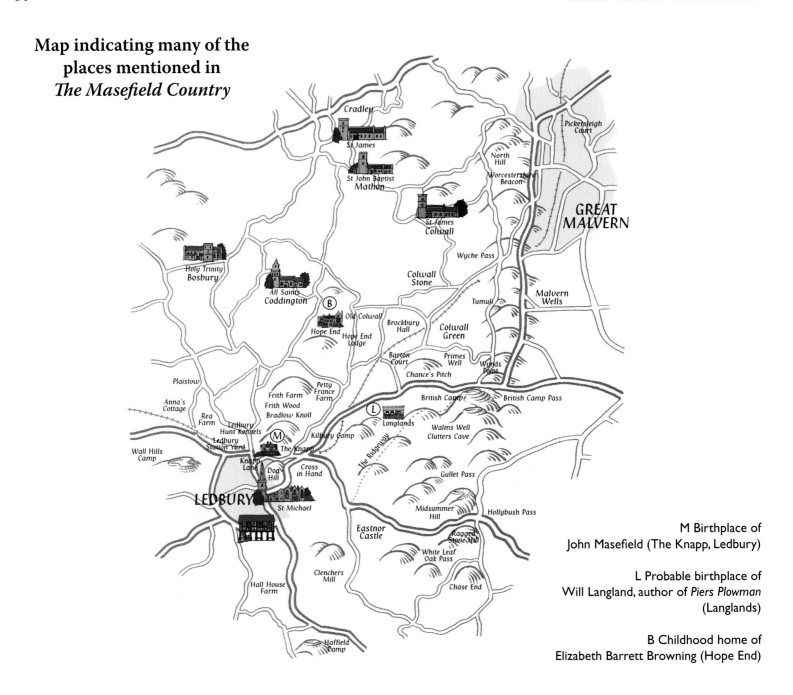

M Birthplace of
John Masefield (The Knapp, Ledbury)

L Probable birthplace of
Will Langland, author of *Piers Plowman*
(Langlands)

B Childhood home of
Elizabeth Barrett Browning (Hope End)

1

This Shire

There is practically no single stretch of Herefordshire landscape that does not rise considerably above the average English standard of physical beauty.

A.C. Bradley

The minor accidents, developed in the making of our earth, are what matter as to our enjoyment of its surface today. A glowing globe at the first, then a cooling one, at last cool enough for water to settle in the crevices of its shrinking crinkles. The lakes and seas so formed to dissolve salt and lime from the crust. Minute living creatures evolve, made right in their bodily functions to absorb this lime, and to build up a protective shell therewith. Dying, they leave their indestructible houses in layers on the sea-bed, to harden in future ages into limestone rock. Elsewhere, the play of the restless waves, driven hither and thither by gales or moon's attraction, grinds into particles the undissolvable rock on which it tosses, to be sand at first, but in ages to come – sandstone.

All this and much more, summed up in the word geology, has everything to do with the type of rocks and of land surface in our particular region, and these in turn decide its beauty and productiveness. So it is that Herefordshire owes most of its special qualities to the accident of being in the Old Red Sandstone, one of the oldest, deepest in bedding, and richest in productiveness – as it

breaks down into clay or soil – of any rock. 'Look, Momma!', cries a child from 'The States' in the Liverpool to Bristol train, passing along the Lugg Valley, "There's red earth in the old country". And red it is to the very borders, and not much beyond, save into the centres of Breconshire and Monmouthshire.

It may be that the encircling ring of lofty hills – Dean Forest, Black Mountains, Radnor Forest, Long Mynd, Malverns – help to shelter it and form a special climate, a bit damp perhaps, but that makes for growth, and hops flourish as in few districts. The valleys of the Lugg, Frome and Teme, are what suit this fickle plant; the Wye, running through the county centre, not so well, and it forms the hop-land limit, so that hardly a hopyard (they are never 'hop-gardens' here), is to be seen west or south of this most beautiful of all English rivers. Even though Gloucestershire blends imperceptibly into our county, and there are hopyards down the Leadon to its borders, my kinsman, Harry Hill of Dymock, found when he planted a new hopyard there, that he possessed almost the only bit of hop ground in Gloucestershire.

Top left: A barrel of local farm cider being delivered to
the New Inn, Pembridge
Above: A horse in the shaft of a cider mill
Left: Best dish of dessert apples, Fruit and Flower Show 1897

So it is with apples. Kent cannot beat us for quality and colouring of dessert fruit, nor Devonshire (the only other old red county) for cider apples. Brecon and Radnor come to us for apples or cider of quality.

It is a good wheat-growing county, and the special breed of red-bodied and white-faced cattle evolved in the rich pastures of the local rivers has developed such a contented sturdiness of digestion and well-doing in these great beasts, that no other strain can compete with them on the plains and rough pastures of South America.

With the changes in geological formation which seem to come close at the county borders on most sides, these qualities change too. Radnorshire is a county full of mountain beauty, but its Silurian formation, older than the Old Red, grows scarcely any fruit or wheat, and no hops, and it is a great-coat colder as soon as one passes the border at Stanner, on the road to New Radnor. Monmouthshire seems more akin, at least that side along the Wye, down which the Old Red soil runs. Into central Breconshire too, the same formation runs, and again bestows a similar scenery, but not the same hop or fruit growing capacity.

The greatest change on the border is that into Worcestershire, for here the boundary was decided – before man was here – by a great fissure opening in the cooling and shrinking earth-crust, this filled up with primal molten rock pressed up from below. Then, after age upon age of wear, convulsion, and changes, a core of hard basaltic rock stood up as the Malvern Hill Ridge. On the Herefordshire side of this is the undulating land of Old Red, with that poor kind of limestone called Cornstone standing out as low hills, for it is a bit harder than the sandstone, and does not wear down at the same rate.

Mr. A.G. Bradley notes: 'These hills enjoy the rather rare and picturesque quality of being draped in rich woods to their summit, a peculiar and characteristic feature of Herefordshire, beyond all question one of the most beautiful of English counties.' Such hills are absent over the Malvern Ridge, for in Worcestershire the land is almost all on the New Red formation, some intermediate strata being absent, which tends to something like a land of plains. A land of pears and plums it is, to the east of the Malverns, and the folk in its capital claim to be "poor, proud, and pretty". Herefordshire on the west, or Welsh, side of the ridge is said by old Fuller – and the saying has become proverbial – to be famed for wood, wheat, wool and water. The water must be Wye water, for we have no natural lakes, and so Shakespeare makes Fluellen tell King Harry – who was a Herefordshire man, for Monmouth-on-Wye was in our county when Prince Hal was born there – 'All the water in Wye cannot wash your majesty's Welsh plood of your pody.'

The folk too, on the two sides of the Malverns, are not quite the same. Perhaps this survives from those days when the Hwicces or salt-carrying tribe prevailed in Worcestershire, and the Magesaetas people [from Magnis, the Roman town at Kenchester] in the great basin with a ring of lofty hills round it, which we call Herefordshire now, from the 'city of the army-road' in its centre [from *here*, Anglo-Saxon for 'army'].

The scope of this book only permits a rapid glance at one of our four Herefordshire *W*s – wood. It is an oak-land, and some of the finest oaks in England have been grown on that ridge and district running from Merbage [Merbach] to Orcop Hill. All, or almost all, our old cottages were built of oak timbers, with just enough stone foundation to come above ground. First the great chimney stack (this of stone), at one end of a cottage, right in the centre for a large house. Then timbers to form the walls were prepared with mortice and tenon to peg together in rectangular pattern, for no nails were used. These timbers were the walls' structure, and held up floors and roof. The filling of the panels between was of wattle (basket) and mud work, although when that decayed brick took its place. The townsman's notion that the timbers were built into the solid brick walls for the sake of ornament is wrong for, in a genuine old house, all the filling-in between the timbers can be knocked out and the house – an open framework – still stands.

The great Norman timber hall of the Bishops Palace at Hereford has still its main timbers holding up the roof, as built just before 1188, although much hacked about, and the curved timbers (two

The cask yard at the rear of the Imperial Brewery in 1892.
To the left is the spire of All Saints Church.

Part of the roof of the 12th-century Bishop's Palace

Wooden pump maker (Mr. Barber, from near Kingsthorne)

to the half circle forming the arcading) required a plank four feet nine inches wide to cut them from, for the said arches are twenty-two feet across.

The craft of turning wooden dishes and platters, once in general use, has vanished long ago. In my own days that of coopering and making casks from our native oak has disappeared. At my father's brewery there were in the yard great open stacks, like chimneys, some twenty-five feet high, of cleft English oak put to season for the coopers to make up into casks. The woodmen cleft and sawed them in the rough and right sizes for staves and heads of kilderkins and barrels and so on, each piled in its stack. With the vanishing of the coopers have gone also many locally made domestic implements, the wooden cider-bottle, the washing tub, the scales to weigh the butter and the churn to make it; the stable bucket too was always of wood and is not well replaced by galvanised iron. When I photographed the Old Bell Inn in Holborn before it was demolished to make way for Gamage's store (Gamage was a Hereford lad, by the way) the stable was still used, and there in the yard was the wooden bucket of water, waiting to bait the nag of one of the last of those who came to town on horse-back.

Clogging survives, for the alder (orle is its local name) is a native wood growing along the banks of the brooks. They are Lancashire men who come down to do it, lodging in a cottage near, and working in a little white tent pitched where the trees are felled by them. It is not 'finishing work', but just sawing to length, cleaving the logs to pieces of right size, and finally roughing out with a lever draw-knife. Then the rough wooden soles are piled in open chimney-like stacks, just like the coopers' stuff was.

Quite gone is the maker of wooden pumps. The craft ran in families: the Edwards, the Jones's of Weobley, (Thos. Jones, Pumpmaker was the sign on their house), the Barbers of Sutton. [In an 1891 Directory Henry Barber of Lugwardine is the only pump-maker shown of this surname. He was also described as a well-sinker.] I met old Barber in the street lately, let out from the workhouse for a day. He had come down to cadging in town, but only about fifteen years ago I photographed him at his skilled work near Kingsthorne. It does take skill to bore a large hole down the centre of a 12 or 15 foot trunk, starting at each end, and with such accuracy that the two bores meet in the centre. All the piping down to the water in the well was of tree trunks fitted with taper nose and socket-joints which had to keep tight. These lower sections were usually of elm timber as that wood does not rot in water, but the pump-body above ground was of oak with iron fittings.

The woodman's craft, whether felling, cutting into cord-wood for fuel, or hauling, is all skilled work, and when so many joined up in the Great War and the wood industry became important, it was the young women who filled the gaps in this last-to-be-expected industry for them. It took just twenty minutes for a forestry girl I watched to fell and clean up a fine young oak tree; she had a few weeks' training in a forestry-camp at Wendover.

Hurdle-making fortunately survives, and uses just the coppice wood available from the growth of uniform size which constitutes our Herefordshire 'woods', cut down about every fifteen years. Very large indeed are some of these woodlands, and in at least

Girls sawing logs during the First World War (around 1915)

Hurdle-making at Wellington

Hurdle-making at Rea (now Rhea) Farm, one and a half miles north-west of Ledbury.
The farm is a large, rambling early to mid-17th century building.

three – the Haugh Wood, Whitcliffe Wood (in which the Earl of Bridgewater's children got lost, giving rise to John Milton writing the masque *Comus* and producing it in the hall of Ludlow Castle, where the poet was staying), and Bolston Wood, where the fallow deer run wild and breed, strays from some deer park a generation or two back. In one of these woods I was hunting for a 'moat' marked on the map, but not easy to find, and suddenly on an obscure track, found my shoulders going into a strong hoop – a deer-snare set by poachers. A farmer in the Ludlow train related how he shot such deer that came in winter time to his homestead for food, as by the common law of England he was entitled to do, for a wild animal is the property of the first man who reduces it to his actual possession. The 'game laws' of course define the exceptions to this bit of common law. Hurdles for deer, by the way, have to be much higher than those shown in the view of the Rea Farm, otherwise they would be jumped. And it is cleft-oak again which makes the tall picturesque deer-fences round our parks, each alternate pale shorter than its neighbour.

To get back to hurdle-making; the nails (with large mushroom heads) used to be hand-made, and I remember trying my hand at one of the shops in Nailer's Row; old Hacket, the last of the Kington nailers, showing me how to point, half cut-off, and bring down the heavy head of the foot operated 'Oliver' to dub the hot end of the rod into a broad head. At Weobley was the sign 'Wm Jones, Nails and Spades Sold Here'.

The multitude of poles formerly used in our hopyards is a disappearing feature which greatly added to the picturesqueness of the countryside in this, the second largest hop-acreage county in England. Twelve to fifteen feet high, they were all grown in local coppices, and each season were newly 'pitched' close together in the hop-rows, being the only support for the hop-bines to climb. A bare forest of sticks until the tender tendrils crept from the ground in spring to climb them. Then greener and greener, until in full flower. Then came the busy picking season, a more picturesque scene than the harvest in vineyards. The bines were cut at the base, and the poles pulled and laid over the picking cribs. During the

Hopyard poles stacked, Ledbury district 1934

Hop-picking (from *Hereford, Herefordshire and the Wye*)

Two photographs of a Herefordshire hopyard
with the hops growing tall in the background

Stripping bark for use in the tan-yards, an important industry in Herefordshire. The tan-yard in Church Lane, Ledbury, would have created a strong smell in that part of town.

winter the hopyards were dotted with wigwam-like stacks of the poles at regular intervals striding the ploughed furrows between the rows of plants, now hidden in the ground. The wire work which has almost superseded all this consists of far fewer but heavier poles in wider intervals like telephone poles, with cross-bar at top and two strands of horizontal wire, there being one line of wire at foot. The hops do not climb the wire, but up perpendicular strings threaded up and down between the wires. Poles and wires remain on the ground all the year round, a rather ugly prediction for next September's crop. And the poles, alas, seldom come from native coppices, but are imported.

Bark-stripping is another woodland industry in our shire, but sadly lessened in importance since all the local tan-yards have closed down, for modern quick-tan methods in large centres take the place of the old 'three-months-in-the-pits' plan. Early in May it begins, for you cannot strip the bark from the tree until the sap begins to run up the trunk. Larger trees are stripped after felling, but coppice-oak has the main trunk done before felling, the men using rough woodland ladders to get high up. Heavy knives for ringing, and queer long 'irons' with thin spade points to wrench off, are the tools used. The bark goes straight to the station now, but one used to see great 'bark-ricks' at certain depots, where merchants stored it ready to sell throughout the year, to large tanneries in London, Edinburgh, and so on. Then on May 29th, the top of every ladder was decorated with green branches, for was it not Oak Apple Day, or Royal Oak Day when King Charles was protected from his enemies by these same oak branches? And go down the street if you dare without a bit of oak-leaf in your coat.

Ash was the wood greatly called for towards the end of the Great War, and in the few years after, for it is of all British woods the most elastic and best suited for aeroplane framework, although steel will probably supersede it. Our woods grow splendid ash. An old industry using bent ash-wood was chair-making and the illustration shows a native one with arms of perfect comfort. But the turners' chairs, rather stiff and upright, made and used in all

Ash chairs at the Old House, Hereford

parts of the county (a lathe used for shaping the parts) were more frequent. At Ledbury, 50 years ago, the sign 'Carless, Chair-maker' was to be seen in the Homend, and a few were made in Bosbury up to the war by the Clissop family. The making of wooden hoops for large casks is another ash-wood industry which (on and off) has centred at Hereford, and here too a modern works for roughing out the ash frames for tennis-rackets has sprung up. Both these last involved steaming the ash before bending into the curve. Cleft wood, that is, split with the grain, is essential, that the fibres which give the toughness may not be severed. The 'cleaver' is an ancient tool in the county, and it is not confined to that form with which butchers split down the meat carcasses. I like to remember the inn sign for 'The Axe and Cleaver' at Much Birch.

The rabbit catcher outside the Unicorn Inn at Weobley – note the nail-maker's sign above the door, as mentioned on page 71. (William Jones, the landlord, was also a nail-maker.) The negative for this photograph is in a poor state, hence the speckling.

2

Laureate Land

In the hearty land where I was bred, my land of heart's desire.
John Masefield

The sharp ridge of the Malvern Hills is not only the boundary of that eastern strip of Herefordshire which was the home of our three poets, but was the cause of its peculiar beauty. This is because the push-up through a long crack of that heat-softened rock which now forms the hard-core of basalt constituting the Malverns, also brought about an upheaval of all the rock-stratifications to the west.

So it is that there runs a very irregular group of hills parallel with the Malvern ridge, about two or three miles west of it. The stratifications of these are all at a steep angle pointing towards the Malverns, and when ill-fated Jim Gurney (whose tragedy is told in John Masefield's *The Widow in the Bye Street*) was helping to move the 'muck' out of the cutting alongside the tunnel in the Ledbury station-yard, before tipping it to form the new embankment which made a rail-line along the course of the old canal, he found the layers of stone on edge in ridges, like the stone paving of a causeway climbing a steep mountain.

The Malverns dominate the district. The three main-road passes crossing them, The Wyche, The Wynd's Point (British Camp), and The Hollybush, are all led up to by a network of roads winding irregularly through the foot-hills of our laureate land.

The cutting in 1884, at the eastern end of the great excavation near the railway station at Ledbury, exposed in section the fossiliferous strata below the 'Old Red Sandstone' called the 'Silurian System'. The excavation was part of the construction of the Ledbury to Gloucester railway known as 'The Daffodil Line'.

Bosbury Cross – a rare survivor. Following the orders of Parliament in 1641 and 1643 to destroy all crosses, the Parliamentary forces were sent to mutilate the cross at Bosbury, but the vicar (Rev. G. Wall) pleaded for it successfully, provided that the words on one side, 'HONOUR NOT THE X', and the other, 'BUT HONOUR GOD FOR CHRIST', were engraved on it. (The photograph was taken in 1917.)

Ledbury itself, a market town of some 3,400 inhabitants, is the centre point of our district, and the only town in it. The area is practically that of the Ledbury Hunt, whose kennels, mentioned several times by Masefield, adjoin the station. The hunt is naturally cut off from most of the Worcestershire plain by the barrier of the Malvern ridge, although it extends over the Hollybush Pass towards Tewkesbury. The pack hunts the country round Dymock, and our area runs well into Gloucestershire, the boundary of which is only about two or three miles south of Ledbury.

There are rather more villages about here than is usual in Herefordshire, where many parishes possess fine churches, but (contrary to the invariable assumption of London journalists) no collection of houses forming a village. Colwall is the largest village but of modern growth, and away from the old church. Dymock is old and compact, as is Bosbury, a place of exceptional interest with its old churchyard cross with original head, and the separate tower to the church – another instance is at Ledbury, thus two in this district out of the seven separate towers of Herefordshire. Cradley and Mathon are both compact unspoilt villages, and perhaps the few houses near Eastnor Church might constitute a village.

Prehistoric man had been busy round here, as witness the large collection of flint flakes which friend John Ballard got together, and I induced his widow to give them to the Hereford Museum. And thus there are a fair number of earthwork camps, probably of the Bronze and Iron Ages. Two of these are on the Malvern Ridge, the Herefordshire Beacon, or British Camp, having perhaps the boldest and strongest earthworks (next to Maiden Castle in Dorset) in the kingdom. It was to this that Langland looked out from his birthplace, and refers to in the opening of *Piers Plowman* as the Tower on the hill, in which dwelt Truth.

Midsummer Camp is also a fine one, on the Malvern Ridge, and both these have been investigated. Between the British Camp and Ledbury is a pretty little earthwork called Kilbury Camp which, like scores of others, was probably a protective enclosure for flocks or herds. Why is it that a military purpose is always assumed for anything known by the name of Camp?

Another small camp on a hill-top (as are all the others) is to be found at Haffield [Donington Parish], and John Masefield in his childhood looked out to Wall Hills, a rather large camp, and, it may be, imbibed his oft-expressed interest in past generations of dead men. All the camps I have named are in Herefordshire.

Tumuli are scarce in the district. I can only name two, these standing on the knife-edge of the Malvern Ridge opposite to Malvern Wells and (as usual) they are sighting points to which old tracks were directed. Standing on one of them I saw, precisely aligned to my feet, two stretches of the present roads towards Upton, these fragments being successors of ancient tracks.

There is one intriguing prehistoric monument on the ridge near to the British Camp: a small artificial cave in solid rock called by local people the Giant's Cave (a name indicating folklore originating in prehistory), which the guide books call Clutters Cave, from a dirty modern 'hermit' who settled in it. Close below this, in a hollow (Herefordshire side), is a rough unworked stone (a local woman told me it was the 'lid of the Giant's cave, fallen down the steep slope') called the Shew Stone, and also the Sacrificial Stone.

With the above exception, however, there is scarcely an example yet noted of prehistoric stone or menhir. I have not the slightest doubt that one originally stood at the present site of Colwall

Clutter's Lane leading over the Malvern Hills with Herefordshire Beacon to the left and the Giant's or Clutter's Cave to the right.
The 'Sacrificial Stone' below the cave is illustrated on page 46.

St Mary's church at Kempley in Gloucestershire is noted for its
12th-century Romanesque frescos.
The village still holds an annual daffodil weekend.

Stone, on the main road close to Colwall Station. A roadman I talked with, in the Yew Tree Inn at Colwall Green, told me that a giant in his cave on Malvern Hills saw his wife carrying on with another chap down in the valley and threw this stone at them. It is a familiar type of tale always indicating a prehistoric object. But the present 'Colwall Stone', a flat table-like block, is said (in an old manuscript unearthed by Mr. Allan Bright) to have been brought down from a quarry on the hill with an ox-team by Francis Shuter in the late 18th century for the milkmaids going to work in the morning to rest their pails on. It certainly (in my judgement) must have superseded a smaller traditional stone there at that time. One small unworked 'mark-stone' of the type which in other districts I know to mark out the ancient tracks, I have noted on the high road just below the Hollybush Pass where Wain Street impinges; but any others are undiscovered as yet.

Moats are plentiful, chiefly at old mansions and homesteads. Almost all have been altered in mediaeval times to protect a house, but many I think originated in an earlier period. Castle Ditches, of which a sketch can be seen at the Hereford Museum,

The sketch of Castle Ditches, the earlier home of the Cocks family before Eastnor Castle was built. It was demolished in 1814 to make way for the new lake.

was the moated seat of the Cocks family, it was demolished for making the artificial lake of Eastnor in 1814, the impressive new Eastnor Castle, on an adjacent site, becoming then the family seat.

The parish churches at the places I have named are almost all fine ones, with many remains of ancient interest, not 'restored' into new structures, except perhaps in the case of Eastnor. Students of old churches are only too painfully aware that in the case where plenty of money is forthcoming:

> Satan finds some mischief still,
> For architects to do

Ledbury is a partial instance of this.

A delightfully unspoilt church is the old partly used Norman one at Kempley (Glos), two miles west of Dymock. This week I found the fields all round it clothed with golden patches, the daffodils overflowing into the graveyard where they grew wild everywhere, not however keeping the country-folk from laying great bunches of them, and of primroses, on the graves in this, their golden garden of peace. It is in the heart of the daffodil fields, not as easy to find as the blatant new church a mile or more away, but its mediaeval wall-frescos and porch, Norman door, arches and roof, well repay the effort.

Pre-Reformation churchyard crosses, or rather the remains of them, are at Cradley, Mathon, Coddington, Colwall and Bosbury, the last with the original head – saved under romantic circumstances from the Parliamentary soldiers about 1642. Others just outside the district I have defined are at Bishops Frome, Putley, Much Marcle and Great Malvern. There are no old wayside crosses hereabouts.

I will not attempt word-pictures of the attractiveness of the landscape of the district. It possesses an ideal grand-stand for its survey – the ridge of the Malverns, the footways along which average little short of a thousand feet in elevation and thus look over the undulating wooded orchard county of Hereford to its further limits. It is a memorable achievement to secure

Top left: Much Marcle Cross, with an original shaft, but the head is missing.

Top right: Coddington Cross has had a modern Latin cross added to the shaft.

Bottom left: Putley Cross has a shortened shaft, but the head is a 13th-century original, although much broken as is apparent in Alfred's photographs of 1929. It has Christ on the cross on one side and the Virgin and Child on the other. The side niches contain St. Andrew and a bishop.

an evening of clear visibility, and standing on the mountain ridge which bounds one edge of the county, to see right across it to the still more lofty level mountain-range – the Black Mountains – which for fourteen miles or so bound it on the other marge. Then, to the right, the ring of limiting hills or mountains coming round by way of the Radnor Forest, the Shropshire Long Mynd and Clee Hills. Within the basin, the slightly wooded hills of the county, with rich cultivated undulations between. The Wye is too far away to get a glimpse of its course.

On foot along the ridge is the ideal way for seeing this, the approach rail-station points being Great Malvern, Colwall or Ledbury. But for motorists, (and how inferior this is for prospect viewing), there is ideal provision in the high level motor road which comes round the Herefordshire side from North and West Malvern by The Wyche, and on to the Wynds Point under the British Camp, as this is comparatively level and averages a height of 800 feet. The high point of the ridge by the way vary from the 1395 feet of the Worcester Beacon to the 835 feet of the Herefordshire Beacon. The vista over the Worcestershire plain does not compare in beauty; for although there are the Cotswolds, with Bredon Hill, the advantage of three towns (Worcester, Tewkesbury and Gloucester), and bits of the course of the Severn to pick out, the rather dreary level plain makes the view flat compared with the rich undulations of Herefordshire.

To be quite frank, it is more the topographer in us than the artist that takes us to the tops of hills. For real beauty, the valleys, orchards and pastures win every time. In my life-long memories of this bounteous laureate-land, there comes to mind the Easter-time sights of the daffodil fields in the district from Kempley through Dymock and Pauntley. The down-turned, golden-bells on long stems, peeping out from grass and briar to the roadside itself and in the field hedges. The sea of short-stem blooms covering field after field with cloth of gold, or seen in the distance as a gleaming patch on a hill-side cleared of woodland. Or the glimpse of a pool in some woodland park, with the dancing bells in separate clumps at water's-edge under tree shade.

These are our golden moments of spring, not without its short-comings of hardness and wiry tree-twigs, which do not form leafy masses of light and shade, as they do later on. I can also pass over the glare of summer, for seeing our land, although this too has many phases of beauty. Harvest-time and autumn are the right seasons to sense Herefordshire. Then comes completeness. The rows of corn-stooks on the stubble. The wagons loading up for the rick-yard. The partly stripped hopyards with their hum of many voices, and thin wisps of blue smoke where tea is being brewed between the rows; the pickers carrying the cribs to an unpicked yard from one just stripped. The red-cheeked apples on the trees, or mingling their fallen fragrance on the ground with autumn-scented leaves. Later, the orchard-harvest of fruit, heaped up for cider-making under the trees. The soft haze over all this fullness. Then in fortunate seasons, days of glorious late October sunshine on woodland, hill and hedgerow, all a-glow with brilliant changing tints.

All lovers of this country find their way beyond these hills to the basin-like dips or disguised valleys which lie on this side of the Malvern ridge. They go by choice to that hollow land on the way to the Hollybush Pass of which Masefield has so well given the spirit in his youthful poem *Tewkesbury Road*; a basin which retains traces in its deer park, and castles on ancient sites, of having once been part of that Malvern Chase which goes to the other side of the ridge, and concerning the boundary of which, between it and the Bishop's Chase in the corresponding basin about Colwall, there was such a long dispute between the Red Earl and Bishop Cantilupe. You pass the Cross-in-Hand to get to either of these two basins, the name a survival from those old days when a felon, having taken sanctuary, had been ordered by the King's Coroner to 'forswear the kingdom', and take the nearest highway to the coast, being protecting by walking '*cruce in manu*' – cross-in-hand. This, like all such named spots, is at a road junction and probably had some kind of shelter for the criminal, to whom it might mean death to depart from the highway, where alone he was protected by his sign. The same junction is on the way to the Bishop's Chase at Colwall, separated from the other dip by that buttress-neck of land leading up to British Camp Pass (its old name I think was Bursters Cross), and you have to climb the dangerous Chance's Pitch to get to the last place by road. The ancient private road by Eastnor, called The Ridgeway, is another route providing an engaging approach or descent to the Malvern ridge at this end.

One can go other ways to Colwall Chase – up the steep Knapp Lane from the Homend, near the station, over the neck between Dog Hill and Bradlow Knoll, and by devious twisting roads, perhaps finding yourself near Petty France, or being deluded by a sign-post and getting to a cul-de-sac at Old Colwall, if you neglect the indispensable one-inch map, for motoring maps of smaller scale will not help you.

And now for the chief reason why this special strip of country deserves a chapter to itself. It dawned on me as I listened to the organ-like voice of the Poet Laureate returning thanks at Hereford on October 23rd, 1930, when the Mayor of that old city bestowed its Honorary Freedom on John Masefield. Here are points from an address which held us all as in a spell:

> I am linked to this County by subtle ties, deeper than I can explain; they are ties of beauty. Whenever I think of Paradise I think of parts of this County. Whenever I think of a perfect Human State, I think of parts of this County. Whenever I think of the bounty and beauty of God, I think of parts of this County. I was born in this County … I passed my childhood looking out on these red ploughlands and woodland and pasture and lovely brooks, knowing that Paradise is just behind them.

Ledbury is the key-note of this land and provided Masefield with both inspiration and subject-matter. Its plan is like that of several market-towns I know – Hereford, Leominster, Bromsgrove, Amersham for instance – an open market having been, at some early time, established in the wide part of some main track. A row of shops springing up down the centre; a covered market house added in line with them. Then other houses built on either side of the main road, forming two narrow lanes on each side of the trading buildings.

Then, perhaps a century ago, these ways became too narrow for the traffic (one of them was called the Butchers' Row both at Hereford and Ledbury) and to widen what had now become the centre of a town, the middle septum of houses was pulled down, leaving the market-house standing, thus providing so wide a street that it almost amounts to a square. At Hereford and Leominster, the demolition of the beautiful market-house followed, but at Ledbury it fortunately remains, the upper chamber being the Town Hall, supported on eighteen chestnut pillars from trees cut down in the Bishop's Chase at Colwall, providing an open covered market below, as seen in my picture. The main street of the town is long and straight, in three portions, the Homend, the High Street, and the Southend.

On market days Elizabeth Barrett, in early girlhood, could have seen farmers and labourers come to town in their smocks, those old-time over-alls embellished with a country-bred stitch and pattern of puckered-up beauty, poorly imitated by needle-women today. John Masefield was just in time to see one or two as a rarity. By 1900 the smock-frock was no longer worn in Herefordshire.

John Masefield receiving the Freedom of Hereford in 1930, when his speech inspired Alfred to write *The Masefield Country*

View of Ledbury from Dog Hill in 1930

The town lies on a side-sloping plateau alongside the park-like tree-clad valley of the Leddon [Leadon], here more brook than river, which runs parallel with the Malvern ridge towards Gloucester. The side streets dip gently to the west down to the little river, and on the other side, in early morning shadow, there climb steeply the several lanes and tracks over the crumpled ridge which overhangs the town.

Dog Hill lies opposite the Homend, and is perhaps the chief feature of the landscape; it is clothed with a wood (now a town-park) to its summit, and in the same line to the north, about opposite the station, the point of the more lofty Bradlow Knoll rises to about 700 feet and, as seen in the picture of Rea Farm [on page 70], makes a feature in the landscape. More to the north, past the Frith Wood, the hills continue, going by Wellington Heath to Hope End and the Lovers Leap beyond. The beauty of these indented hills, with 'such nooks of valleys lined with orchises, fed full of noises by invisible streams', is done justice to by Miss Barrett in *Aurora Leigh*.

A pleasant town to approach when coming from the north, giving an impression of spaciousness and yet compactness. Slightly down-hill one descends the Homend to the bottom of the dip at the Market-house, and then the wide High Street slightly up-hill to the top crossing where, half closing up the vista, is the many-gabled timber mansion of the Biddulphs, in which Prince Rupert lodged when he occupied the town with his cavalry in 1645 and inflicted a minor defeat on a Parliamentary force.

At opposite ends of the High Street are the two road-crossings, the Lower Cross and the Upper Cross, as they are still called, the Upper one the more recent, for its branch to the west is New Street, although old enough to be already called 'new' in a document of 1232; the branch to the east, now the main road to Worcester, with an appropriate motor-scout at the narrow corner, was originally only a minor track.

The Lower Cross, at the Market Hall, was the original and prehistoric crossing of tracks. To its west lies the Bye Street, a peculiar name, to be found also at Hereford until the city fathers there in their early Victorian fatuousness changed it to Commercial Street.

Ledbury Market Hall on market day looking north, in 1884

Bye Street, Ledbury, with the steeple of the parish church in the background

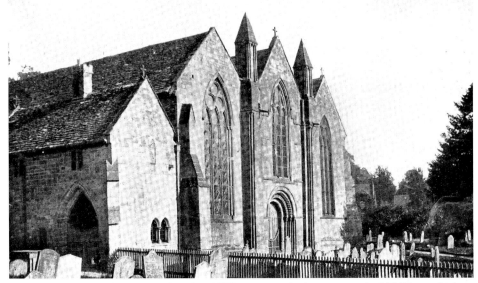

The west front of Ledbury church c.1878, prior to the 'restoration' of 1895 to which
Alfred objected so much. The plain Latin cross seen on the gable was
replaced by a wheel-pattern cross.

To the east goes the picturesque narrow Church Lane, where carts cannot go nowadays, and even in the last century, when Mutlow's tannery in it was in use, the oak-bark had to be shot down at its market-house end and carried up in baskets. And yet, when Prince Rupert made his dashing little victory, it was (so Lord Biddulph says) part of the main road to Worcester, going on through the churchyard. It has that striking feature, so often seen in old towns, that a church tower is exactly aligned in its vista, as my photograph shows. No one had ever attempted to explain such a feature, of which Offa Street, Hereford and Grope Lane, Shrewsbury are other instances, both too narrow for modern streets, until I showed in my *Early British Trackways* that they were surviving bits of old straight sighted tracks.

I used this photograph of Church Lane to illustrate the point, but had not then worked it out. Only recently I have found, by exact work on the 6-inch Ordnance maps, full co-operation of this being a bit of such a prehistoric track by the numerous confirming points on its alignment. It is precisely east and west, to equinoctial sunrise and sunset, and passes over the summit of Eastnor Hill, then on to lie on the northern ditch of Midsummer Hill Camp. Here, since I named this as an old track, expert excavation of this camp has been made, and in the exact alignment of Church Lane, and in its direction, Mr. I.T. Hughes found the unusual feature of no less than three 'paved ways' in the camp ditch, of three successive periods, as they were on the top of each other, with earth between. He was unable to decide on what these meant, but made as one suggestion "that the ditch may have been used at some time or times as a track". I have in many other cases found lined tracks coming to the edges of hill-top camps, and often showing as a notch (and therefore a visual directing point) on the sky-line. John Masefield describes such a fact at Badon Hill Camp [in his poem *Badon Hill*].

Ledbury is, to a great extent, a town of timber-built houses and several of these, as Ledbury Park (Lord Biddulph's House), the Feathers and Old Talbot Inns, were covered in plaster when I first knew them, but are fortunately now stripped to show the picturesque crossing timbers. Many others are faced with brick fronts, which is perhaps the prevailing aspect of the streets, for it is a brick-making district providing buildings of a subdued quiet red, not with the yellow unbaked appearance of London clay bricks. Stone houses are not in evidence, and in fact most of Herefordshire is badly off for building-stone.

The church is a large one, as are all those in settlements of any size in Herefordshire, and like our other local ones has traces going back to at least Norman times; this one is perhaps chiefly in the Decorated period. But looking at my photograph of the west front, taken before the 1895 'restoration', I fail to see why new tracery designed by the architect had to be inserted. Neither old nor new windows are of the period of the original Norman structure of this front which has still Norman door and turrets surviving. [Alfred noted the traces of two small windows in the west face, but these had been lost at a much earlier date.] And why the plain Latin Cross finials should now be replaced by the wheel pattern ones so dear to the soul of the modern 'restorer' I also fail to see!

The separate church-tower, standing some yards away from the main buildings, is the only separate tower in our county which has a spire, as the other six instances have square, pyramid roofed towers. The nearest one at Bosbury is of stone, as is that at Richards Castle, but those at Pembridge and Yarpole are mainly timber-built, and of Scandinavian influence. At Holmer, the upper half is a timber structure.

Looking eastwards along Church Lane, Ledbury

If this view looking up the town, framed by the pillars and spandrels of the Market-house, be examined (see opposite), there will be seen on the left a large copper kettle hanging as a sign over a shop front. It is an old customary sign of an ironmonger and brazier. It still hangs there and apparently had done so for a century or more, for after I photographed it, in about 1884, and showed a print to John Ballard, he related this story:

Long ago, when the penalty for felony was transportation 'beyond the seas', and accompanied by forfeiture of all the felon's personal property to the Crown, a man who was connected with this shop was so convicted, and transported for a term of years, probably to Botany Bay. He served his sentence. The day after his return, he quietly planted a ladder against the iron bracket from which the kettle hangs, and taking off the kettle-lid, took out the bag of gold coin which he had deposited there before his conviction.

The legend of St. Catherine of Ledbury, perhaps just as good a saint as if confirmed by the authority of Rome, I will give in the words of a local farmer acquaintance who was recently telling me what he knew of local traditions:

Do you know Mabel's Furlong? They say that when Catherine Audley was on pilgrimage, she had Mabel with her, and they heard the sound of bells thereabouts. They were not far from Hazel Farm – and Catherine sent Mabel forward to know where it was, and it came from Ledbury Church. But that, and the belfry was all locked up, so the bells were ringing of their-selves. So Catherine said 'Here I shall stay'.

And do you know of the box that Catherine left to the people of Ledbury, with a lot of valuables in, and strict orders that they were not to open it till it opened of itself, and then they would see. But if they opened it afore, they would never prosper. But the people were too greedy to wait, and they did open it. And that is why the people born and bred in Ledbury don't seem to prosper, but die off, and do no good for they-selves.

I cannot say that I have noticed this last fact, and it was probably coloured by the temporary pessimism of 1931. Catherine of Ledbury, however, was a real personage and did (in 1313) give up her earthly possessions and settle as a recluse, or anchoress, in a cell. Both Wordsworth and Mrs. Barrett-Browning refer to her in verse. She is a different person to the St. Katherine of Alexandria who gives her name to the Almshouse in the High Street founded by Bishop Foliot in 1232.

The chapel in the church, said to be dedicated to Catherine Audley, has most beautiful windows of flowing, Decorated tracery studded with the characteristic local ornament of that period, the ball-flower. Mabel's Furlong Lane is still marked on the 6-inch Ordnance map, and with a footpath continuing it, points directly at the church, while nearby is a plot of land called Catherine's Acre.

The copy (in oil) of Leonardo da Vinci's *Last Supper*, which was the altar-piece at the church, now hangs on a side wall there. It was painted by Thomas Ballard of Ledbury, who had two sons, John Edy Ballard, grocer and inventor, and Tom Ballard, art-master in London. Both, whom I often met, were delightful and interesting characters, not caring a brass button about money or the making of it. They were the only people I have known who could tell of two grandmothers of theirs who were twins.

This Tom Ballard (the second) has been rather fully sketched and appreciated in Henry Festing Jones's *Life of Samuel Butler* as 'very tall and thin, with aquiline features, clear grey eyes, and straggling beard and moustache', 'one of the best men I ever knew, certainly the most charitable, very poor, but always ready to share

View through the arches of Ledbury Market Hall in 1884, looking southwards

his last shilling with any artist or model who was hard up'. 'He was an able painter but quite without ambition.' 'He had apples, he had them sent to him from his home at Hillway, in his pocket, which he munched as he walked along the streets. He was extraordinarily well read – indeed he was always reading in the street.'

In a Worcester paper, about the time of his death in 1921, a friend gives further notes of Tom Ballard, as:

> a rare sample of a generous unselfish man … an artist of no mean kind. … The love of painting coupled with the ability to help some poorer friend or relation out of the inadequate payment he often received – this was his life. … Most of the scene-painting in the Gilbert and Sullivan operas was done by Tom Ballard, often, strange to say, without taking the full kudos of his toils, but working under another who received most of the credit, and the cash … A brilliant conversationalist, humorous and full of wit, he was a delightful caller.

The passing of the Hereford and Gloucester canal through Ledbury seemed to me to give it a touch of romance. Canals may not seem romantic to present-day people, but when they came as a new idea at the end of the 18th century they were called by the general term of Inland Navigation, and looked upon as bringing up goods from the sea to inland pastures, meadows and villages. A new race of men evolved to dig them, and these were called navigators, or later on navvies. I have heard the full name used in Ledbury half a century ago. 'Just then two navigators, slightly inebriated, came rolling down the street.' Great burly men, with a slow rolling walk something like a sailor's, wearing short jacket, characteristic neck-cloth and spacious corduroy trousers, hitched to the body by three tight straps, one round the waist, the others below the knees, leaving the upper part bagged up a little, the forerunners of plus-fours. They have changed to another type now but lingered on for a time to make the earlier railways, which came so soon after to supersede the waterways. The early name the 'cut' clung to our local canal. To me as a small boy, walking down along a bit of it on my way to school, there was romance in the canal people and all their trappings. The touch of jazz decoration about the boats and fittings, that checkers pattern we used to see on the posts of inn-doors being a favourite, the buckets and boat-poles and hooks all a bit different to such things elsewhere, and all gaudily decorated if at all possible; the loud-voiced women, the only women at that time working on equal terms at the same jobs as the men, steering, swearing, shoving, working the locks. The children, taking their turn at the tiller, or walking alongside the old draught-horse; the wonder how there was room for all to sleep in the tiny cabin.

The canal was brought to Ledbury from the Port of Gloucester in 1798. Then about 1830 there was a movement to extend it on to Hereford, it being pointed out that it would bring down the price of many goods; coal for instance then being 25 [shillings] a ton at Hereford, but only 17 [shillings] at Ledbury. So it was dug (some of the bridges bear the date 1844 and Stephen Ballard was the engineer) and opened in the thirties [actually opened to Hereford in 1845], alas, only to be bought up forty years later by a railway company, to smother a competing, cheap, if slow means of goods transit.

Early in 1881, hearing it was about to be closed (the embankment at the Ledbury Station end of the new Ledbury-Dymock railway having already started), I persuaded another young boating spark, (Ted George, whose father had founded a timber business at the Canal Wharf at Hereford), to come with me on a two days' final water-trip by canoe along the whole length to Gloucester. A very jolly trip it was, chasing down ducks who flew and flapped in terror at the strange invaders, diving through tunnels with a small boat's lamp, to give light, carefully balanced on the bow, and shouting songs to keep our spirits up in the case of that long weird tunnel (1¼ miles) at Oxenhall, where we could not see the other end and were paddling into the blackness of night, with the water washing the walls on both sides, for in this one the tow-path went over the top of the hill, and the canal-men had to 'leg' their barges through by pushing with their feet against the roof. This however was on the second day's trip after passing Dymock and the belt of daffodil country about Boyce Court where, as I wrote in my half-century-ago account of the trip, 'they spangle the hedgerows and literally carpet the meadows, and even on the bank their graceful flowers bend over to look down into the natural mirror of the water'.

At Ledbury dusk was falling when we landed at the wharf, left our canoes in the warehouse there, and walked up Bye Street for a night at the Feathers.

Where the canal used to be crossed at the bottom of Bye Street by a bridge with the lock below, now stands the railway bridge with the line in the old canal bed. Near this bridge Masefield pictures his 'Widow' peering and waiting night after night for the return of her son, whose body was lying in quick-lime in the yard of Hereford Gaol. And on the bridge is the little house in which lived old Robert Edy (his name-plate on it lingered until lately), a lawyer and grocer, to whose business his nephew the inventor succeeded; in this house too, died his other nephew, Tom Ballard, one of the best judges of old masters in London, an artist theatre-decorator, who painted for D'Oyly Carte the 'ancestors' in that scene of Ruddigore where they step down from their frames; a man so kind-hearted that he would empty his not well filled pocket to any tale of woe.

Hereford and Gloucester canal – the House Lock at Newent *c.*1880

The Ballard Family

I find that the Ballard family is to my sketch of Ledbury as known to me something like King Charles's head in Mr. Dick's memorial: it will crop up. Here then is an outline linking them together, with perhaps the advantage that those to whom 'two grandmothers who were twins' is a bit of a puzzle, as I have found when telling the tale, will get a needed explanation.

There is a pretty old timber-built house, called the Abbey House, on the left (just above the wheel-barrow in my picture) coming down the Homend towards the Market-House, which can be known by a narrow gabled wing (was it a powder-closet above?) projecting into the street; it used to have an ancient vine festooning its walls.

Here, in the late 18th century, there lived with their parents an attractive pair of sisters, identical twins Charlotte and Ann Baylis. Few people could tell the two apart, but the family doctor always pooh-poohed this and said that he had not the slightest difficulty. So one day the parents, on his visit, put this to the test. The two girls, dressed as usual identically, went out of the room, and were to return one at a time.

'Which is this one?' was asked at the first entering.

'Why! Ann of course, that's quite easy to see', the doctor said.

'No, it's Charlotte', the gleeful answer came. Now the old doctor had always known Ann, without telling anyone, by a tiny faint birth-mark on the side of her dainty nose. The girls had found this out, and it being early summer, Charlotte had taken a ripe strawberry, and with the two bright faces reflected side by side in a glass, had fabricated a mark to match her sister's, then going in first.

They both married. Charlotte in 1795 married Phillip Ballard, a solicitor of Malvern, and they set up house-keeping in that beautiful old house, Pickersleigh Court, near the Link, a many-gabled, half-timber farm house, unspoilt when I first knew it. Of the children of this marriage, three talented brothers come into this narrative – Thomas, Stephen and Phillip. Thomas Ballard had training as an artist in Paris and settled in Ledbury.

Stephen Ballard, born at the Link, was the engineer, with more solid enduring work to his credit than all the others. After his canal building he was associated with Brassey, made the first railway in Holland, carried the Great Northern railway across the marshes of Lincolnshire, and constructed the tunnels through Dog Hill at Ledbury and the Malvern Range. He was living at Colwall in 1851 and there built, in concrete, his house, The Winnings, where his family were all born. One can always tell Stephen's houses by their generous eaves.

His estate ran up the hillside at Colwall, and the sturdy old engineer elected to be buried up there by the mouth of a ventilating shaft to his tunnel. This curious instinct for burial on a height was shared by such men as Cecil Rhodes, Robert Louis Stevenson, and Lord Carnarvon, being handed down from early man and his customs.

Fate, a few years later, played a strange prank with this fancy, for the shaft fell in, blocking up the tunnel, and the enlarged funnel-shaped apex was so near the grave that this only escaped being carried bodily down below by a few yards.

Stephen, besides other able sons and daughters, left a son Fred Ballard, for many years chairman of the Malvern Hills Conservators, promoter of an Act of Parliament for conserving these hills, and in this matter coming off best in the battle of words with an imperfectly informed critic, George Bernard Shaw. He is now [1931] Chairman of Herefordshire County Council.

Phillip, the other son of Phillip and Charlotte Ballard, had a strange career. He, like Thomas, was trained as an artist in Paris, and then learnt china-painting at Worcester. Afterwards he was one of the chief artist-decorators at a porcelain factory in Madeley, in Shropshire, which existed from 1825 to 1840, and the wares from which [Coalport] are eagerly collected. After this ceased, he was secretary to the Hereford and Gloucester Canal, and he experimented with lithography at the Ledbury Press. Returning to Hereford, he was a valued adviser in the 1858-63 restoration of the Cathedral, and in his old age was murdered in bed by two burglars at his house, The Knoll, Tupsley, close to the city.

Now to get back to the other twin grandmother, Ann Baylis. She married Thomas Edy of the Frith Farm, Ledbury, and they also had as issue a family of character: Thomas, whom I knew at the Frith; Robert, the lawyer and grocer – both these brothers dying bachelors. Then there was a sister, Ann Edy (what a trim short name it is), who married her cousin Thomas Ballard, the Ledbury artist. He did not make money at his art, and as a widow, she carried on business as a tanner at those tan-pits in the Bye Street which were already derelict when I first knew Ledbury.

Her two sons (coming into this narrative), were John Edy Ballard, the inventor, and Thomas Ballard, the London art master. These were the delightful people who had two grandmothers who were twins.

As to John Edy Ballard, how the memories crowd on me. Our first encounter in the marketplace, his tall figure, long, eager, bearded face, his accusing finger pointing at a silver Denarius I was wearing mounted as a tie pin (bought from Lloyd, a poacher close against the Roman Town at Kenchester), his exclamation,

The Homend looking south, with the timber-framed Abbey House (built c.1600) on the left just beyond the Horseshoe Inn

'Oh what a shame!' Not that he ever wore collar or tie himself, except under pressure from a despairing wife, for some special visit. The frequent calls after that at the inventor's den at the back of the shop, for his hovering about the counter was almost limited to market-days. The new thing each time, now the machine he made for grinding, perfectly spherical, those pith balls which, in the days of the influence of the Royal Polytechnic, used to dance up and down between electrified plates. The other elaborate machine for slicing perfectly parallel, from rock-fragments, thin micro-sections. The model of that simple hand-adjusted arc-lamp worked with a battery, which John Browning of the Strand advertised in *Nature* for many years, which my friend designed. His harmonograph, with penduli swinging across each other, for recording on paper the graphic curves corresponding to musical notes. His models (John Masefield had been there and noted one of a ship), perhaps the most interesting being bone toys made from their dinner bones by French prisoners-of-war at Bristol in the Napoleonic wars. The fire-side coal tongs which really would hold tight the bit of coal; the experiments with a lawn-mowing machine which combed up the grass before cutting it, just as a barber does with a comb before he plies the scissors. The pleasant teas in the parlour, the youngest of the family, now an engineer, in a high chair, another now art-master at Folkestone. Then his keen interest in other investigators, how in 1890 when I brought him a sample of my just-invented meter for gauging light in photographic exposures, he characteristically tried it out under difficult conditions, namely, on the beautiful ball-flower windows of St. Catherine's Chapel, not exposing until after the chimes had played for nine o'clock on a fine summer evening, his report on the success of this, and comment in the words of Tom Moor:

> The best of all ways to lengthen our days
> Is to steal a few hours from the night, my dear.

Of course, like a true inventor, he had always in his pocket some 'whim-wham or mustard mill to catch cuckoos in', as he would explain to wondering or inquisitive boys. I am not sure that they were not there as a plant.

A local friend who had, with Ballard, a mutual fondness for old watches, usually had one or two to show, each wanting to go one better. One day, when this was at its keenest, John Ballard made his preparations and came across his friend in the town. One after another they pulled out their treasures to compare, pinchbeck, silver, or tortoise-shell cases, all variety of movements. The friend had come provided with seven 'tickers', but John won the trick by producing from his pockets three more (ten in all), when the other had played all his cards.

After his mother's death, he was able to retire to the Abbey House, in the Homend (the pretty home with a garden steeply climbing the bank at the back), where were born a century and a quarter earlier his twin grandmothers. You can still see his telescope on a stand in the windowed nook looking up and down the street. You may know the house by the flight of many steps up to the front-door. Rest his memory.

3

William Langland

Out of the mist into the light;
O blessed gift of inner sight.
The past was faded as a dream;
There come the jingling of a team.

John Masefield

Back in the seventies, as we – active youngsters – were planning at the breakfast-table a good day's walk along the Malvern ridge, my father said, 'If you should be going by the British Camp, call and see Peter Pocket who keeps the inn there. He was the best man at my wedding.'

So, taking train to Great Malvern, we ascended the town, climbed up behind the Unicorn Inn, which was kept then or soon after by Timothy Trigg, continuing steeply up the green way to the hill-ridge, then to the left along it, crossing that cutting called The Wyche, because the salt-folk used this pass when bringing their wares from Droitwich towards Dean Forest. But we still kept along the ridge, finding a track on the west sheltered from the keen blast which that day poured over the knife-edge. So at last we came to Wynd's Point where, at the road junction, a small road-side inn, called the British Camp, stood in the neck, almost overhung with that great hill called either the Herefordshire Beacon, or (from the ringed trenches encircling it) the British Camp. Over the inn-door we read the legend – 'Peter Pocket, licensed to sell ale, beer, cider,

wines and tobacco'. Outside the door – it was a small place, not expanded, as now, into a pretentious hotel – sat in a chair Peter Pocket himself, a quiet little old man of the Ham Peggotty type of face. In response to our approaches he just grinned, and remembered my father as an early chum of his younger days, for whom, somewhere on the Gloucestershire border, and probably under pressure, he once performed the said service. No more could we learn. That's all I know about Peter Pocket, whose name, like that of the aforesaid Timothy Trigg, is fact not fiction. They would not have crept into this record did not their names show a survival of the old English liking for alliteration, so well marked in the *Piers Plowman* poem. We still find this in the Simple Simon, Peter Piper, 'tattered and torn', 'shaven and shorn' of our early nursery tales.

We little knew as we went down Chance's Pitch towards Ledbury, making for the short cut to the station, that we should pass the birthplace of the man who wrote *Piers Plowman*, and the half-acre strip against the highway which he ploughed so diligently. Still less could we guess, as we climbed the banky road between Bradlow

A view of the place Alfred believed to be Langlands, near British Camp in 1929

and Dog Hill, to come down Knapp Lane for the station, that at the new house we saw before us as we turned from the lane into the Homend, there was soon to be an infant 'mewling and puking' in his mother's arms, whose destiny would be Poet Laureate.

No-one, when reading Langland's great poem of *Piers Plowman*, will fail to find some passages of real poetic beauty – as this:

Thus I went wide-where	walking alone
In a wide wilderness	by a wood side.
Bliss of the birds song	made me abide there
And on a lawn under a linden	I leaned awhile
To listen to their lays	their lovely notes
The mirth of their mouths	made me to sleep
And mid that bliss	I dreamed – marvellously.

The shrewd and carefully detailed observation of the life of a fourteenth-century English man or woman worker on the land is unsurpassed. Listen to what might be a present-day account from a worker amongst the very poor.

The neediest are our neighbours	if we give heed to them,
Prisoners in the dungeon	the poor in the cottage,
Charged with a crew of children	and with a landlord's rent.
What they win by their spinning	to make the porridge with,
Milk and meal,	to satisfy the babes, –
The babes that continually	cry out for food –
This they must spend	on the rent of their houses,
And for themselves	suffer from hunger,
With woe in winter	rising a-nights,
In the narrow room	to rock the cradle,
Carding, combing, clouting, washing	rubbing, winding and peeling rushes
Pitiful it is to read	the cottage-woman's woe,
Ay, and many another	that puts a good face on it,
Ashamed to beg	ashamed to let neighbours know
All that they need	noontide and evening.

Many the children	and nought but a man's hands
To clothe and feed them,	and few pennies come in
And many mouths	to eat the pennies up

I am quoting this poem throughout in the 'Everyman' translation (by Mr. Arthur Burrell) into modern English, because those of us who are not students of early or middle English feel pulled up by the unfamiliar words and mannerisms in the original. Another difficulty is the loose way in which the writer drifts from describing real persons and happenings to allegorical ones. The mystery play was to Langland the basis of the art of poetry, but his sturdy common sense was constantly breaking away from such artificial structure to real happenings, and then we find him getting back into the conventional form.

The fact that *Piers Plowman* is not a book completed and sent to press by a certain date, but a progressive manuscript, written in several stages during 36 years of the author's life, the back parts several times revised, and the whole only published by copies made by scribes, makes for confusion and want of unity. Professor Manley has surmised it to be the work of several writers, a theory however thoroughly demolished by that fine student of English mediaeval life, Dr J.J. Jusserand. *Piers Plowman* is therefore none too easy to read, and it has not been made any too accessible to the ordinary student.

What I can say about Langland's connection with this bit of countryside is all based on researches given in Mr. Allan Bright's *New Light on Piers Plowman*, which exploded the error that the poet was born at Cleobury Mortimer in Shropshire. I followed this work for a paper to the Woolhope Club, and (as I have done often for fellow members of the club) I went over this long familiar ground and sought out and photographed the illustrations (showing Herefordshire Beacon, Langlands and Primeswell Bourne) to illustrate the subject. Mr. Bright has I think, in conjunction with Canon Bannister, fairly proved their case, and as it is supported by such authorities as Dr Jusserand and Professor R.W. Chambers, I here follow it.

William Langland, therefore – referred to [in a 15th-century manuscript] in Trinity College, Dublin as William de Langland – is stated to be the son of Stacey de Rokayle of Oxfordshire, a gentleman tenant or retainer of Lord le Spenser, the Despensers being also at the time lords of Malvern Chase. William was illegitimate, born about 1332 at Longlands (Langlands), in Colwall parish but only two miles from Ledbury and quite close to the boundary of Malvern Chase. He was never able to take his father's name, a resentment to this being shown in his book; but he received a good education at the Priory school, either of Great or Little Malvern, and according to Stowe, also went to Oriel College Oxford, this not confirmed although his writings show signs of academic training. He was ordained an acolyte to Bishop Trellek at Bromyard Church in 1348 under the name of Willelmus de

'On a May morning on Malvern Hills, a marvel befell me ...' This is a view of Raggedstone Hill, which stands above Little Malvern Priory.

Colewell, this releasing him from the position of a serf to that of a free man. He never took higher orders, and although he evidently worked on the land at times in his earlier life, his further life's work seems to have been clerical.

Mr. Bright finds some evidence for supposing that he acted as tutor to a certain 'good knight', and surmises this to be James de Brockbury living at the moated manor house of Brockbury [half-a-mile SE of Colwall Church], the position apparently described in the poem as 'A court, clear at the sun with a moat, the manor all around' ; the 'tower that holds truth is set above the sun'. It is a fact that 'the tower that holds truth' – the Herefordshire Beacon – is against the sun from Brockbury old moat during the morning. No trace of this old fortified manor house remains, the present trim farm house and its pair of hop-kilns being on a new site alongside.

Some incidents of a personal rupture between William and the 'good knight' are to be found in only a few copies of the poem. This possibly arising from an attraction of youth between the young tutor and the young wife who, with her step-children, he taught. So, about 1355, before *Piers Plowman* was written, William, a young man of 23, went to London. There are indications that at first his occupations were irregular, not clerical, with some knowledge of a life bringing in certain damsels named (in the poem), Lust of the Flesh, and Covetousness-of-Eye; but later in a fairly long life, he settled down to the usual occupations of the lowest order of a clerk in holy orders, that of an acolyte, and was therefore free to marry, which would be forbidden to a deacon. So marry he did, but presumably not before the first text of the poem was published about 1363, and from certain allusions his wife seems to have come from the town society I have previously hinted at.

The years rolled on, with poverty and broken health for Will Langland, who tells us much of his difficulties:

> Thus I woke, God wot   where I dwelt in Cornhill,
> Kit my wife and I   dressed like a loller,
> And among the London lollers little was I set by.

A loller was little better than a street beggar, and he gets a living as best he can:

> I live *in* London   and I live *on* London
> The tools I labour with   to get my living by,
> Are the Lord's Prayer, my Primer,   my Dirges and my Vespers.

There comes a vision of God's pardon for all who honestly work and, only half awake, his mind drifts to boyish days on the hillside:

> I through their words awoke   and waited about
> And saw the sun in the south   sinking at even,
> Meatless and moneyless   on Malvern Hills,
> I mused upon this dream   and went upon my way.

The whole Gospel story passes in procession before the tired old mind:

> Then piped Peace   a note of poetry and sang;
> 'After sharpest showers   most shining is the sun;
> There is no warmer weather   than after watery clouds,
> Nor is love sweeter   nor are friends dearer,
> Than after war and wrack   when love and peace have
>   gotten the victory.'

He dreamed how Righteousness and Peace kissed each other:

> Truth then trumpeted and sang *We praise Thee, O God*
> And Love luted in a loud note *See how good and joyful a*
>   *thing it is (for brothers to*
>   *dwell together)*
>
> Till the day dawned   these damsels danced,
> And men rang in the resurrection
>   morning.   With that I woke
> And called to Kitty my wife   and to Kalot my daughter
> and said: 'Arise, do reverence to God's resurrection,
> Creep on your knees to the cross and kiss it for a jewel.'

I write more from the point of view of one who finds deep interest in the character and life of one particular bit of our English countryside, and its connection with our poet, than in the attitude of a literary critic. So let us seek out Langland's rooting in this beautiful bit of England.

Mr. Bright clearly proves the former error made in attributing a birth-place. It evidently arose from a copyist's blunder in Crowley's printed edition of *The Vision of Pierce Plowman* of 1550, where the word 'Cleybirie' is mistakenly written for 'Ledbirie'. Cleobury is 23 miles from the Malvern Hills, whereas the early writer (and those who copied him) state that the birth-place is 8 miles from the Malvern Hills, a distance approximately right for Ledbury. Then, there is not the slightest local corroboration for Cleobury and it has no place named Langland near, it being noted that we are writing of William *de* Langland.

On the other hand, about half-way between Ledbury and the Herefordshire Beacon, there is a parcel of land called Longland, the older form being Langland, on which an old house stood a century ago, and which was divided into cultivation-strips, as was the land where Piers ploughed his half-acre. My photograph shows how the deep indentations of the British Camp earthworks on the Herefordshire Beacon stand 'eastward against the sun' from the spot, the new cottages shown being on the site of the old one. And it is on the old highway, as Piers describes.

Let us note the topography named in the opening lines:

But on a May morning	on Malvern Hills,
A marvel befell me	– sure from Faery it came –
I had wandered me weary,	so weary, I rested me
On a broad bank	by a merry-sounding burn;
And as I lay and leaned,	and looked into the waters
I slumbered in a sleeping,	it rippled so merrily,
And I dreamed – marvellously	
I was in a wilderness	wist I not where,
And eastward I looked	against the sun.
I saw a Tower on a hill	fairly fashioned,
Beneath it a Dell,	and in the Dell a dungeon,
With deep ditches and dark	and dreadful to see,
And Death and wicked spirits	dwelt therein
And all between,	between the Hill and the Dungeon
A fair field	full of folk
Rich and poor	all manner of men,
Working and wandering	as in the world we must.

Now to identify this passage with the local facts. There is a deep grassy hollow or dell on the side of this massive hill, which Langland truthfully terms a mountain, in a following passage where Truth descends from her Tower on the summit. The hollow sides are so smooth and steep that in my younger days I discovered their capabilities as a tobogganing slope, a board obviating disastrous contact between communicative green grass and tweed trousering. The high road to Ledbury crosses the tail of this cwm and, steeply below, a copious spring boils up. Pewtress Well it is now called, from (as Mr. Bright tells me) a former parish curate, but its old name was Primes Well. From this a fast running brooklet goes

Langlands, near British Camp in 1929, with the British Camp earthworks outlined against the sky

down the little wood and along hedge-rows. At one spot, where it turns to the right, it is in a beautiful open meadow bank, which in my search I recognised as the 'broad bank by a merry-sounding burn'. Indeed there had long been a local tradition to that effect. [The photograph alongside shows] where the dreamer lay, and could look up at the steep hill, with its cast-up entrenchments and hollow side above him. A Norman stone-tower no doubt at that time crowned the summit, for in a last-century excavation there, not only the Iron Age pottery of those who dug the ditches and made the camp were found, but also relics of mediaeval life.

I think it unsafe, however, to labour to find too exactly the 'Fair Field' and the dungeon down below it. For it was years later, when in London, that the poet dreamed and wrote of the folk who seemed to pass in a hazy procession; hermits and bishops, jesters and jugglers, beggars and pilgrims, sergeants-at-law and clerks, butchers and bakers, masons and miners; mainly of his London experience, drifting across a 'field' which is only a dreamer's stage having his boyhood's country background.

Pewtress Well is dammed up now for factory water supply. The story of this seems worth the telling. A mineral-water firm of standing wisely resolved to build a new factory at the Malvern Hills – for a name-title tells in commerce. The Colwall side of the range was selected, a site bought close to the station, and the factory walls began to rise. The water supply was to be from an Artesian well, no doubt of water in this hill-side of springs! So it was sunk deep – no water, deeper still, no water yet. At last, at a great depth, a bountiful supply gushed up and overflowed – it was brackish and useless. I used to see the overflow running down to waste in the station yard. So in the emergency, water from a well-known spring above Colwall village (probably the original Cole Well) had to be bought from a neighbouring landlord, rumour says at a generous price. This is why, after some years, a new supply was sought, and Piers Plowman's 'merry-sounding burn' piped across the parish to be gassed and bottled.

From the land springs Piers Plowman's knowledge of its cultivation, and the poet selected his name well. What a versatile man

Primes Well, now called Pewtress Well, is believed locally to be the most likely spot for the dreamer to have lain.

was this keen common-sense Englishman with his dream habit, and gift for verse. It is right that Mr. Arthur Burrell, the editor of the 'Everyman' edition, looking at him from the scholar's point [of view], remarks that Langland 'was as much of a town man as Dr. Johnson'. But we country-bred men know that Mr. Burrell is wrong in saying that 'he never approached Chaucer in the out-door Englishman's appreciation of field and forest and stream', and in speaking of his 'vague and rather intellectual love of the country and its sights'. It is perhaps not much of the chase but of the farm-labourer's life that Langland tells us, from that full knowledge with which he is saturated from birth. Knowledge, too, which applies today. What town-born man could tell us of this form of roguery, based on the common use of land without fences?

If I went to the plough	I pinched of his half-acre
A foot or a furrow	of my neighbours land
If I reaped I would reach over	or bade them that reaped for me
Seize with their sickles	what I never sowed.

It happens that a Ledbury man some years ago told me this story:

> I don't often go into the County Court, but I looked in at an action about a dispute in which men representing the parish of Colwall (in which Langland was born), accused a well-to-do owner of property adjoining common land of pinching a strip of it in rebuilding his fence. When the said owner had given his evidence and called his first witness, the judge addressed him:
>
> 'Now you may call fifty witnesses to support your case, but I shall know that neither they nor you tell the truth. And for this reason – I knew this to be a difficult case, so I went myself beforehand to the spot. I saw with my own eyes your new line of fence, and I saw also the stump of the tree which the people of the parish say marked the old boundary. And I saw that it was, as they assert, a yard or two within your new enclosure, and I saw other signs of your having stolen this bit of the people's land. The verdict against you with costs.'

Truly the craft of the ploughland is in the bones of Langland. When he refers to a poor man's meal, a prosperous man's eating; we get it all in detail, not merely the type, but exact quality. Where else can we know exactly what kind of bread was eaten in the fourteenth century? Piers tells us that all who could afford it had 'wheaten bread', 'white bread', 'fine bread' or 'stamped (kneaded) bread'. It follows that the general rule for the miller was, then as now, to separate the outer bran from the white inner part of the grain, which alone makes that digestible fermented spongy structure which we know as bread, and which no other grain (save rye), will produce in such open cellular form. So we find in his annals of hard days waiting 'till Lamass time' when 'I hope to have harvest in my croft', that even Piers has to put up with 'loaves of beans and bran, baked for my little ones'. The bran, be it noted, could only have been procurable if taken out by the miller when preparing white flour for more prosperous folk. We learn too in this record that the very poor had to put up with 'bread with beans in it', or 'barley bread', coming down even as low as 'horses bread' and 'hounds bread', whatever these were made of.

I have been curious, as one brought up in what is now a cider county, to know how that drink stood in those days, and here again Langland clearly gives the information, when he classes it with scarce wines.

No nectar and no cider	and no costly drink
Shall moisten me	or slake my thirst.

It was not until much later that the local drinking of cider became general in our county, when Evelyn could write in his *Pomona* of 1629, 'By the noble example of my Lord Scudamore and of some other public-spirited men in these parts, all Herefordshire is become in a manner but one entire orchard.' What a contrast between the 'costly drink' of Langland's time and its status in the nineteenth century when, here in Piers Plowman's land, the farmers made the 'men's cider' in great casks, and allowed to their workers seldom less than two quarts a day, and a gallon in harvest time. True it might be a bit 'peart' at times, as John Masefield's Nan remarks in pouring some out to her sweetheart, but a cider drinker does not mind that. 'We likes it to cut the phlegm of a morning', said one of them.

Probably the town man regarding (wrongly) cider as naturally a sweet drink would say to the 'men's cider', 'Peart isn't the word!'

Many years ago when the old *Clarion* newspaper had several young journalists of outstanding ability – Robert Blatchford foremost – one of these (Neil Lyon, I think) gave his impressions, in a series of articles, of a trip on foot across country which included Ledbury. There he found himself in the evening at a decent little inn called the Ring o' Bells. Here, in a diversion, let me say that this does not

A horse and tumbril carting a load of cider apples in the snow to the Pomona Works at Withington to be transformed into cider

mean a peal of bells used to call the parish to church, but a set of six (in a few cases two more are added on a bracket to make the octave) hung in a hoop over the shoulders of the leading horse in a team drawing a wagon, so as to give warning in narrow lanes of their approach. Well, in the top room of this inn, the *Clarion* man found that many of the lads and lasses of Ledbury were having a dance. He was not loth to join in, and partook of the refreshments. The more solid of these he did not record, but the cider, contained in a bucket in one corner of the room to be dipped into with small mugs by the dancers, did seem to make an impression. He reported it as not unpleasant, but that later on he formed an idea that he had swallowed a spiral staircase which, as he noted, was not a nice experience to an unsuspecting Fleet Street man. But let me do justice to today's cider of commerce, and say that the spiral staircase attribute is in this quite absent.

It was only in years of cider scarcity that my father's brewery had a trade for 'Harvest beer at 6d. a gallon', reminding me of the comment I once heard on 'such tack' by a man who was asked by his master how he liked the drink. 'Well sir, it be just right.' 'But what do you mean by "just right"?' 'Why, if it had bin a bit better we wouldn't a-had it, and if it had bin a bit wus we couldn't a-drunk it, and so it be just right.' This was in the last quarter of last century, and now with a minimum wage act, the custom of drink allowance has ceased.

To dwell upon the practical religion and social politics which are the backbone of Langland's book would be outside my subject. He seems to have reached at a bound the standard expounded, let us say, in the actions and published code of one or two of our present London Police Court magistrates. The practical touchstone of Pier's creed is 'Does he work honestly?' And this applied without a touch of favour to every class, from King, magistrate and knight, to labourer and beggar. If anything, he is most severe on men of education, such as lawyers, and those like himself in holy orders.

None sooner ravished	from the right creed
Than cunning clerks	that con most books,
None sooner saved	none surer in creed
Than plowmen, shepherds	and poor common folk.

How advanced and courageous a pioneer this country-bred man was, can be judged by the fact that for several hundred years after his time, clerks of his own standing could escape extreme punishment for their misdeeds, if they were able to recite in the dock a few passages illustrating their learning. Even Ben Jonson escaped hanging by this 'Benefit of clergy' provision. A sweet, but common-sense, charity coloured all his social planning, even to beggars, if down and out.

Far more weighty than anything I can write is what Dr. Jusserand has to say in comparing the two great writers of mediaeval England, Chaucer and Langland:

> *Piers Plowman* ... is a unique monument, much more singular and apart from anything else than Chaucer's masterpiece. It is more thoroughly English. Chaucer is at his best when describing individuals. The author of *Piers Plowman* concerns himself especially with classes of men, great political movements, the general aspirations of the people ... He does not describe them simply to add picturesque touches, but to express what he feels, and show how the nation should be governed and morally improved. He is not above his time, but of it; he is not a citizen of the world, but a thorough going Englishman and nothing else.

William Langland died, obscure and in poverty, in London, about 1399.

4

Elizabeth Barrett

Honour, anger, valour, fire;
A love that life could never tire,
Death quench, or evil stir,
The mighty Master
Gave to her.   Robert Louis Stevenson, *To His Wife*

The callow enthusiasm of a lad for the verses of the only then known local poet, his declaiming bits of *Aurora Leigh* and *The Cry of the Children* at the town debating society in those Victorian days, his opportunities for visiting the first home of his heroine; these incidents and others necessitate relating fragments of my own life.

Shot straight from school into one of several producing businesses founded by my father, part of my work in early life was travelling for his brewery and spirit business. This took me to Ledbury, long enough ago to enable me to talk to old people who knew and remembered the Barretts before they left in 1832.

About 1873, therefore, occupying the day in business calls at most of the Ledbury inns – practically all the smaller ones – I delighted to leave to the end of the day a mile-and-a-half walk past Beggar's Ash, and by footpath across a meadow skirted by a brook, to be noted later by a poet not then born as 'one of two which rise in my green dream in Paradise', then to be welcomed as a friend by kindly folk who kept a little beer-house at Wellington Heath. Here I heard much talk among work-people of the pulling down of an old mansion close by, at Hope End, and how a 'rich man from the north' was about to build a new one. It was when walking out in the evening, into this fold in the hills, that I first saw the glow-worms' beacon-light in a sheltered hedge-row, and grew to share Elizabeth Barrett's enthusiasm for the beauty of her countryside.

The house then pulled down was Hope End, where Mrs. Barrett Browning (to give her full married name) spent her girlhood. It lay in a beautiful little closed, or hanging, valley – a 'hope' being the native name for such a valley – opening out in one direction only, towards the plain and chase of Colwall, and was and is an ideal spot for a mansion secluded in its own grounds. Its wooded vistas are in one direction only, towards the Malverns, for nothing can be seen in the direction of Ledbury, two miles away. It was a deer park until Mr. Barrett's time. Three successive mansions are recorded at Hope End, and I am able to illustrate all.

The first, a brick-built box with a chimney at each corner, was acquired by Henry Lambert, by marriage with Jane Pritchard, an heiress who was grand-daughter of one Pritchard, who made money from the now familiar craft of turning wooden dishes. Miss Radcliffe Cooke tells me that she finds in records of Much Marcle that dish turners were established there.

Mr. Allan Bright relates how the daughter, Sarah Lambert, fell a victim to a fortune-hunter, Sir Henry Vane Tempest, of Tong in Shropshire, who, getting wind of a silly young heiress, disguised himself as a gipsy woman and told the romantic girl's fortune on Colwall Green; how next day she was destined to meet, at Colwall Church, her future husband – he of course being at the named place in his own dress and name. It came off as projected and they eloped to Marylebone Church, where they married in 1791. The baronet then claimed Hope End in his wife's right, and turned his father-in-law out of it, before long quarrelling also with his wife and turning her out as well. She tried to see her father, who now lived at Barton Court (then called The Bartons) [extended by Henry Lambert south of Colwall in about 1791], but he refused, and the poor lady had to go to a relation and did not live long. Her ghost is said to have wandered about Barton Court, and people (so relates Mr. Bright) are still afraid to go at night down the Barton Holloway, a deep sunken road just below the Court, where once I saw a large snake wriggle across in front of my car.

Mr. Bright, who now lives at Barton Court (his ancestor having bought and come to Brockbury, close by, in 1699), tells how the young Peytons (of whom more presently) used to shoot at the ghost, and how it was said that twelve parsons with twelve candles tried to lay it in a pond in the grounds. All the candles save one went out, but that belonging to the local parson kept in and it was presumed that the ghost was laid.

The second mansion was that built by Edward Barrett Moulton-Barrett on a site just a bit higher up the valley. The father of our poetess, as a very small boy, had inherited much wealth from his grandfather in Jamaica, his birth-place. The little lad was sent to England to live as a ward with a rising counsellor-at-law, Mr. Scarlett, soon to be Chief Baron under the title of Lord Abinger. To be brought up with many servants always telling Master Edward what a rich and important personage he was, then to come to England and travel about with his guardian on circuit, often in semi-state carriages with javelin men in attendance; to go to Harrow and to Cambridge; then to be straightway married – 'when 18', his son wrote – to have an attractive country place provided and plenty of money, with freedom to build to one's own ideas; what better recipe in those days for the making of a special variety of prig? I leave it to be gathered from Miss Carola Oman's delightful book what a portentous papa Mr. Barrett became to his offspring.

It was in Trafalgar year that Mr. Barrett married Miss Mary Graham Clarke at Gosforth Church, Newcastle-on-Tyne (May 14th, 1805). Elizabeth was born at Coxhoe Hall, Durham, on March 6th, 1806. This house was rented from Sir Henry Vane Tempest, and thus it was that the young husband came to buy, in 1809, the Herefordshire Hope End estate, which his landlord had

Hope End – a print (photographed by Alfred) of the brick-built mansion acquired by Henry Lambert and demolished by Edward Barrett in 1809

disgracefully acquired by his elopement and run-away marriage, at Marylebone, with his victimised first wife. Little could it have been foretold that the baby Elizabeth was also destined to make a run-away marriage from her father's house, and to be married at the same Marylebone Church.

In possession of Hope End, Mr. Barrett at once pulled down the Lambert house, with its pretentious Blue Drawing Room, and built a new one according to his own fantastic ideas. Turkish minarets with solid concrete walls and double-curve cast-iron tops, windows over fire-places, blatant ogee curves over doors and windows, all contributed to what might now be termed a 'Lord George Sanger style' of architecture. For over twenty years this was the home of the numerous Barrett family, for twelve almost 'annual events' were the lot of the dutiful wife, only one dying in infancy. Eight boys and three girls there were, and it is characteristic of the man and his code that the last two boys were called Septimus and Octavius, the girls not counting. Not but what he was a devoted father to all, the favourite being Elizabeth.

Then in about 1832 came a reverse of fortune, resulting in a 'compounding with creditors', who first took a mortgage on Hope End and then, to Mr. Barrett's intense chagrin, for he was still fairly well off, sold it to Mr. Thomas Heywood. The Barretts left the district in 1832 and never returned. The house survived their going about forty years.

The print reproduced here was from the lithographic press at Ledbury, which my friend, John Edy Ballard, had often told me about as being founded by his uncle, Phillip Ballard, in conjunction with his father, Thomas. Phillip made several drawings for this press. Thomas Ballard, too, was an artist and when his widow died, John gave me a small lot of prints from this local lithographic press, chiefly marked 'T. Ballard', but two of them ' P. Ballard'. The Hope End print, not dated ('P. Ballard, Litho.'), was from a sketch by Mrs. Heywood, whose family must have lived there a long time, for her son Col. Thomas Heywood, who was my colonel when I served in the Volunteers in the seventies, and who died at Malvern, sold the estate to Mr. Hewett in 1872.

Hope End as built by Edward Barrett between 1809 and 1815, with its concrete minarets, cast-iron domelets and ogee-headed windows (photographer unknown)

An undated lithograph of the Barretts' Hope End by P. Ballard after a sketch by Mrs. Heywood, whose son Thomas lived there for some forty years after the Barretts left

To complete the story of the three successive houses at Hope End: Mr. C.A. Hewitt, who had bought the estate from Col. Heywood (both were in cavalry regiments), began at once to build his handsome new stone mansion on a site at the head of the little valley or 'hope' (for the name has not its usual English meaning, as several town-bred commentators have assumed), higher up than the old house whose site can now be traced by the stables. The owner was of good family in a double sense, being the twelfth of the twenty children of the Honourable and Reverend John Hewitt, son of Viscount Lifford, Dean of Armagh; and he became a leading magistrate in the district. The house was burnt down in April 1910, and after some years was reconstructed in post-war proportions by the son.

Some years passed by after the old fantastic house of the Barretts disappeared, and I was still visiting Ledbury, although now for the mill rather than the brewery. It was half a century since Elizabeth had driven in the family carriage through Ledbury Market-Place, having left Hope End never to return. But little as the people of the town had seen her, they followed with a touch of local pride her subsequent rise as a poet, and kept alive their memories. The thumbed

In 1872 Mr. Hewett bought Hope End and built a handsome new stone mansion higher up the hanging valley. It was burnt down in 1910.

copy, first edition, of *Aurora Leigh* which I picked up second-hand came from a sale at Ledbury, and although the printed date on the title page is 1857, the written inscription, 'A. Gregg, 1856' (that of a known Ledbury lawyer of the time, or one of his family), shows that someone was on the look-out and bought it immediately on publication. So, about 1884, my Ledbury friend, John Ballard at the grocer's shop at the corner of Market Place and Church Lane (inventor, artistic craftsman and dilettante in heart and practice), often spoke of his parent's recollections of doings at Hope End.

I was told too, how 'Uncle Thomas Edy', who still farmed at The Frith, remembered and could tell of the Barretts. I had met old Mr. Edy at the tea table in the parlour behind the shop, and appreciated the strong steady outlook of the old man. It was he who commissioned 'Uncle Phillip Ballard' to paint and decorate the beautiful jug of the scarce Madeley ware with its landscapes of Ledbury. You can see it, quite lately bought from old Miss Ballard's sale in the little house on the canal bridge in the Bye Street at Ledbury, at the Hereford Museum, and see on it the initials 'T. E.' of the farmer-kinsman for whom it was made.

So at last, in 1889, an appointment was made. A morning walk up the cart-road leading to the Frith Farm, tucked away under the wood which gives it the name, a wood coming down on the slopes of Bradlow. Glimpses of old-time out-buildings, cowsheds, and hop-kilns; breakfast in the spacious kitchen; the old housekeeper Thomas Edy never married waiting on us, but retiring to the back-kitchen. A cold round of beef flanked by a loaf of home-baked bread, perhaps baked ten days ago, but not a bit stale. To drink – a jug of perry, made with Barland and Yellow Huffcap fruit from the trees outside.

Yes, he remembered Mr. Barrett, a nice gentleman, religious too, but not advertising it, just quietly to himself. They were all a clever family. He had seen Miss Barrett about sometimes in her invalid's chair, but not often; they were great friends with the family of Mr. Nicholson Peyton of Barton Court, who had a miniature theatre of marionettes. This I had heard of from John Ballard whose father, Thomas, painted scenery for it, and I had been shown a small backcloth for it, representing Ledbury old High Street with a row of houses, now demolished, down the centre.

Miss Barrett, continued the old man, wrote a prologue for the play, the first poetry he had heard of her writing, and he had a written copy of it somewhere, the Peyton's governess had given it to him afterwards. Young Mr. Peyton, Major Peyton he thought in after years, was long after heard regretting that a summer-house, where he had often played with the Barrett children, had been pulled down.

Then the old gentleman went upstairs to look for the 'lines of poetry', and I took stock of the kitchen – the old family china on the dresser, the polished steel trivet before the fire. A few prints hung on the walls, one frame, however, with its back only showing, and on this chalked the words 'Claims of Mr. Eyre'. This I was told, when Mr. Edy, unable to find the 'bit of poetry', had come downstairs again, was a portrait of Mr. Gladstone (the Edys and Ballards were all traditional Liberals), a great favourite until he was so unjust to General Eyre over that Jamaica revolt affair, when his face had to go to the wall. He was forgiven for that after a few years, and was allowed to see the light again. But when he took up with Home Rule – he went to the wall again for good! So I left the house feeling that feudal influence – of a landlord whose income all came from Jamaica – was not yet extinct.

Walking on to Lovers Bush (the name on some maps is Oyster Hill), a man bark-stripping told me how he had helped to pull down the Barrett mansion, with its cast-iron tops to the domes, and solid thick walls which had to be blown up with powder. 'It would have lasted longer than the new house will now', he said prophetically.

In another visit, this time on a path across Hope End grounds, when the owner was away (for he objected to anyone photographing about the place, and once ordered off the vicar, who was trying to get a view of the house), I met a little old man walking with sticks. He remembered the old house, and how Mr. Barrett would walk into their cottage when they were at dinner, and help himself to a 'tater' off the dish, and say that 'fingers were made afore forks'. The boys would often call in too, and he was sorry when they all left. But they thought of him, though, and left him a box of wooden soldiers. The old house was richly decorated, the drawing-room said to have taken seven years to do, and when Mr. Barrett once showed him it as a wonder, 'He said that if he thought there was such another in England he would pull it down'. Somehow I find a richly decorated blue drawing-room, and a wish to out-do rival rooms elsewhere, featuring in both the rebuilding of the Bartons by Henry Lambert, and of Hope End by Edward Barrett; was it a symptom of similar types of mentality?

In this and another visit, I took in the lay of the land, to use a country-bred phrase, the narrow slightly curved hope, or little valley, the carriage drive in its dip alongside a decayed summer-house with ice-house at the back, the small lake in the wider part, now choked up with great green leaves, water-lilies probably. The faint suggestion of the old Barrett house in the minarets of stables left of its fragments; the steep tree-crowned banks on either side.

Elizabeth recalls it all as she remembered it in her girlhood days, before illness kept her indoors:

> ... past the lime, the lawn,
> Which, after sweeping broadly round the house,
> Went trickling through the shrubberies in a stream
> Of tender turf, and wore and lost itself
> Among the acacias, over which you saw
> The irregular line of elms by the deep lane
> Which stopped the grounds and dammed the overflow
> Of arbutus and laurel. Out of sight
> The lane was; sunk so deep, no foreign tramp
> Nor drover of wild ponies out of Wales
> Could guess if lady's hall or tenant's lodge
> Dispensed such odours – though his stick well,crooked
> Might reach the lowest trail of blossoming briar
> Which dipped upon the wall. Behind the elms
> And through their tops, you saw the folded hills
> Striped up and down with hedges.

(Aurora Leigh)

The lime had gone. But although I saw traces of the sunken lane coming down behind the lodge, which still stands where the drive comes into the cross road for Old Colwall, I have not traced its course, although Mr. Grant, the steward at the Home Farm, who facilitated my visits, told me that he knew it just as described.

I had to take my photograph of the view showing the Malverns (it's all of forty years ago) by climbing the bank, for there did not seem a view of them from where the house stood. Probably Elizabeth did this for the view she describes so splendidly:

Far out, kindled by each other,
Shining hills on hills arise ...
While beyond, above them mounted,
And above their woods also,
Malvern hills, for mountains counted
Not unduly, loom a-row –
Keepers of Piers Plowman's visions through the sunshine and the snow.

(*The Lost Bower*)

Taken above Hope End drive with British Camp in the background – 'Far out, kindled by each other, shining hills on hills arise'

It was the life of a country-bred child, spent in those earliest days; indications at times of wanting to be alone with her own thoughts under the skies.

> To slip downstairs through all the sleepy house,
> As mute as any dream there, and escape
> As a soul from the body, out of doors,
> Glide through the shrubberies, drop into the lane,
> And wander on the hills an hour or two,
> Then back again before the house should stir.
>
> (*Aurora Leigh*)

There is plenty of evidence however, that the budding poetess (her proud father published a small private edition of a poem written by her at twelve – *The Battle of Marathon*) took a lead in the romping play of her many brothers and sisters, especially with the children of their neighbours, the Peytons, at the Bartons, which is alluded to in *Aurora Leigh* as Leigh Hall, the smoke from its chimneys just showing above the trees from Hope End. Mr. Bright writes of the Peyton family from his recollections: 'There were six Peytons: Reynolds; Tom; Nicholson; Beryl, who became Mrs. Selwyn; and Fanny and Rosie. They were very generous-hearted people.'

There were signs too, in one or two poems (as in *The Lost Bower*), of other active country rambles, touched with a child's fairyland imagination, but none of any contact with the little town, or with the life of any workers outside her father's estate.

There are indications, if we regard *Aurora Leigh* as partly auto-biography, as we surely must, that Elizabeth went through a phase of boy-and-girl flirtation in those days – here is the passage:

> Saying which, I loosed my wreath
> And swinging it beside me as I walked,
> Half-petulant, half-playful, as we walked,
> I sent a sidelong look to find his thought –
> As falcon set on falconer's finger may,
> With sidelong head, and startled, braving eye,

> Which means, 'You'll see – you'll see! I'll soon take flight,
> You shall not hinder.'

Ever since my talk with old Mr. Edy, a surmise that one of the Peyton lads was the prototype of Romney Leigh gains strength, though without proof. Was there this slight flirtation with Reynolds Peyton? For Mr. Bright says that he devoted the tithe barn at the Bartons, at one time, to sheltering wayfarers, a somewhat similar thing described with Romney Leigh, who captured Aurora finally by the accident of blindness. Reynolds was 'the lame one' among the Peytons. Mutual memories on both sides seemed to linger.

In her fifteenth year came an accident, a partial spine injury, when mounting her pony, and after this it was a shrinking invalid who passed her days indoors at Hope End.

> I lived with visions for my company
> Instead of men and women, years ago.

So it is written in one of her sonnets. And again:

> I grew up in the country, had no social opportunities, had my heart in books and poetry, and my experience in reveries. ... It was a lonely life, growing green like the grass around it.
>
> (*Letter to Robert Browning, March 20th, 1845*)

Elizabeth, in her girlhood, had made a life-long friend in Mrs. Martin, of Old Colwall, with whom she corresponded to the end. Perhaps it was in the active days she took the old track which, passing an ancient yew tree, goes over the top of the hill to Old Colwall. There was the pony-chaise to take her after the injury, and to friends at Eastnor (Lady Margaret Cocks is mentioned), and at Mathon. It is Mr. Robert Holland Martin writing, from the sign of the Grasshopper in Lombard Street, of this track, and tells me that Mr. Martin came to Old Colwall in 1812, and that his great-niece lives there now. How strange it is, by the way, that at least four great banking families had their ancestors going up to a commercial career from the Ledbury district, and founding banks. The names of the Biddulphs, Somers, Cocks and Martins will be familiar to readers, and deserve fuller treatment in regard to this countryside than possible here. About 1910, when calling at the Yew Tree Inn on Colwall Green, I used to have talks with old Mrs. Pedlingham, the mother of the landlady, who was a maid in the household of Mrs. Martin in her youth, and she said she remembered the visits, or the talks of visits, of Miss Barrett, and of Miss Florence Nightingale. But the visitor must have been Arabel [Elizabeth's sister], not Elizabeth, who never returned after 1832.

The old lady's son, who keeps the adjoining grocer's shop, told me that she delighted in reading, so I asked what kind of books I could lend her. To my surprise she said, 'Anything about history, or old places, churches and castles'.

To return to Elizabeth Barrett. John Edy Ballard used to tell me that his parents always said she disliked coming into Ledbury and seeing people, and was several times noticed waiting in a pony-chaise outside the turnpike-gate (it was at the road junction close to the present station) while her father came on into the town. And this is confirmed by there being no descriptive reference to the picturesque town or the people in it in her writings.

It was as living near the Malvern Hills, or Malvern, that Elizabeth wrote in her letters years after. The outlook of the mansion, the main lodge-gate through which she drove to visit all her friends, all were in that direction. To Malvern also, on the other side of the hills, she drove, two or three times a week it may be, to read Greek with a most desirable friend to whom her father had found an introduction. This was Hugh Stuart Boyd, with whom (and his kindly wife) a real affection developed, kept up by correspondence till the death of the two elder ones. It is a delightful memory, this link of letters between the young girl and the old blind scholar.

> And I think of those long mornings
>   Which my thought goes far to seek
> When, betwixt the folio's turnings,
>   Solemn flowed the rhythmic Greek.

> Past the pane, the mountain spreading,
> Swept the sheep-bell's tinkling noise,
> While a girlish voice was reading –
> Somewhat low for ais and ois.
>
> (Wine of Cyprus)

It is our lovely countryside which is over and over again depicted in her verse:

>   And when, at last
> Escaped, – so many a green slope built on slope
> Betwixt me and the enemy's house behind,
> I dared to rest, or wander ,– like a rest
> Made sweeter for the step upon the grass, –
> And view the ground's most gentle dimplement,
> (As if God's finger touched but did not press
> In making England!) such an up and down
> Of verdure, – nothing too much up or down,
> A ripple of land; such little hills, the sky
> Can stoop to tenderly and the wheatfields climb;
> Such nooks of valleys lined with orchises,
> Fed full of noises by invisible streams;
> And open pastures, where you scarcely tell
> White daisies from white dew, – at intervals
> The mythic oaks and elm-trees standing out
> Self-poised upon their prodigy of shade, –
> I thought my father's land was worthy too
> Of being my Shakespeare's ...
>
> (Aurora Leigh)

Could anything be better done, this poet-memory of her own land, written nearly a quarter of a century after she had left it? Its beauty still lingered, and her girlish optimism in drinking it all in.

> Hills, vales, woods, netted in a silver mist,
> Farms, granges, doubled up among the hills;
> And cattle grazing in the watered vales,

And cottage-chimneys smoking from the woods,
And cottage-gardens smelling everywhere,
Confused with smell of orchards.

(*Aurora Leigh*)

In those after years of exile under Italian skies, deep from her heart came the moan:

I shall see no more those hills and trees which seemed to me once almost like portions of my existence.

(*Letter to Mrs. Martin, December 19, 1834*)

There is little more to tell of Elizabeth Barrett's life as linked up with Herefordshire-under-the-Malverns. Poor Mamma, colourless and complaining, had faded out of life in 1828, leaving Elizabeth, now a woman of 22, the lady of the house. But the cares and responsibilities of management did not come to her, her health was poor and 'dear papa' allowed no financial detail to be shared by his family, even in the wife's lifetime. Household expenses were between him and a well paid housekeeper.

He was a 'queer quist', as we Herefordshire people would say, and had kept from his family the financial losses which, coming a year or two before the end of slavery in Jamaica, cannot be put down entirely to that cause. His upbringing, to early power of purse without training to teach its true responsibility, combined with the slave-owning mind he inherited from generations of ancestors, had produced a mental attitude which was, as years went on, a tragedy for his children. He firmly believed that they belonged to him, body and soul. While in other ways a kind and affectionate father, he absolutely forbade them (to the end of his life, and he lived until 1857) to marry or even contemplate marriage. Three of them in turn, Elizabeth, Henrietta, and Alfred, the only ones married during his lifetime, could only do it by eloping from their father's house, and it is a fact that each, from that day, was absolutely cut off from the self-centred tyrant, who refused to know or communicate with them or their new relations.

You can see a tablet in Ledbury Church recording the burial there of Edward Barrett Moulton-Barrett and his wife, although he was, in the phrase of local society, 'a chapel man', and we do not hear of the family as they grew up entering the said society via the Rectory or Vicarage.

A firm foundation to Elizabeth Barrett's poetic genius was formed at Hope End, although only one volume of immature verse was published before she left Herefordshire in 1832, a woman of 26. Her real literary life came later, and is not within the scope of this record. She tells us that 'poetry has been to me as serious a thing as life itself'. This is to be kept in mind when reading Miss Carola Oman's brilliant historical novel *Miss Barrett's Elopement*, for there the feminine human interest is foremost, and Miss Barrett is rather made to deal in poetry as a ladylike diversion.

Elizabeth does not seem to have come into touch at all with the ordinary people of the countryside, beyond a few on the estate to whom the family showed kindness. Her mother coming from a 'county family' and her father's narrow conventional mind, combined with her own semi-invalid state, cut her off from what a young poet ought to know of real life. There is no indication of her being in touch with anyone or anything in Ledbury. Even her keen mental insight never, I am afraid, made up for this. In *Aurora Leigh*, her poor folk, as Marion Earle, do not ring true to life and, in spite of a good dramatic plot, and much beautiful and intellectual verse, Victorian conventions and ideals are too evident. The 'retirement scarcely broken to me except by books and my own thoughts' was not the best training.

Just as Langland aimed at a social-political influence in his work, so did Elizabeth Barrett. Her *Cry of the Children* was a passionate protest against the disgraceful exploitation of child-labour in factories. It did not fall on deaf ears, and Sir George Cornewall Lewis, Member of Parliament at different times for Hereford and the Radnor Boroughs [whose bronze statue, sculpted by Marochetti, stands in front of Hereford's Shire Hall], took a special pride in using his position in the government to push through, in 1834, a Factory Act dealing with the evil. But her judgements and opinions in Continental politics later in life do not seem to bear the test of time.

Two or three years were spent at Sidmouth in Devon after leaving Herefordshire, and then the whole family settled in London. Years of growing literary activity and reputation followed, but also of serious ill-health with threatened lung-trouble. Then the romantic courtship of the invalid on her couch by Robert Browning, their elopement from her father's house and marriage at Marylebone Church in September 1846, the immediate journey of the poet lovers to Italy, where Elizabeth Barrett Browning was to spend the rest of her happy married life. The birth of a son, 'Penini', in 1849 completed her happiness. He was described later by an observer as 'An Ariel, flitting about, gentle, tricksy, and intellectual'. The unusual household of high thinkers evolved the wicked comment in society about them – 'Then there were but two incomprehensibles, but now three incomprehensibles'. She died, smiling, in her husband's arms, in Florence in 1861, in her fifty-third year.

I heard a literary critic on 'the wireless' recently, giving Mrs. Barrett Browning second place to Christina Rossetti, and it might be a true judgement. I see also a tendency for young readers to find inferiorities in all the Victorian poets to present day ideas. And they too may be right. But I have listened lately to readings, chiefly mouthy and sonorous, sometimes melodious, sometimes incoherent, of modern verse, again on the aether. And after hearing these, I turned up the first of the *Sonnets from the Portuguese*:

> I thought once how Theocritus had sung
> Of the sweet years, the dear and wished-for years,
> Who each one in a gracious hand appears
> To bear a gift for mortals, old or young:
> And as I mused it in his antique tongue,
> I saw, in gradual vision through my tears,
> The sweet, sad years, the melancholy years,
> Those of my own life, who by turns had flung
> A shadow across me. Straightway I was 'ware,
> So weeping, how a mystic Shape did move
> Behind me, and drew me backward by the hair;
> And a voice said in mastery, while I strove, –
> "Guess now who holds thee?" – "Death", I said. But, there,
> The silver answer rang, - "Not Death, but Love".

Then I thought of a little pile of pebbles picked up from Aberystwyth beach and cut by the lapidary there with, by their side, a large fully cut unmounted Brilliant of the first water.

5

John Masefield

Those that I could have loved went by me;
Cool gardened homes slept in the sun;
I heard the whisper of water nigh me,
Saw hands that beckoned, shone, were gone
In the green and gold. And I went on.

Rupert Brooke

Both Will Langland and Elizabeth Barrett were brought up in the country, a mile or two out of Ledbury. John Masefield was a native of Ledbury who came from a family of solicitors of standing, which began in Ledbury with his grandfather George, his father, George Edward, then continuing the practice in partnership with his uncle William.

John Edward (he dropped the second Christian name when he began to write) was born at The Knapp, Ledbury on 1st June, 1878 – the glorious first of June it was long called, after Admiral Howe won the great sea-battle of St. Vincent on that day.

An old farmer acquaintance tells me that, before the Masefields bought the place, he came as an infant with his father from Bosbury way to the old thatched farmhouse which stood on the site before the present pretty half-timbered house (as Victorians interpreted that style) was built in the 1860s or '70s. The name is the original one, signifying that it stood on a 'chap' or hillock. Indeed this is very evident if you walk around the fields between it and the

Leddon, for it seems mounded-up from below. It lies between the station and the town at the north end of the Homend.

From the front of the new house the child looked out across the canal and the Leddon onto the hill-top prehistoric camp of Wall Hills, as the other two poets looked out from their child-homes to the great British Camp. And who can say that the spirit and feeling of long-dead men on these hills did not bring them some message?

A field away, the canal runs towards Gloucester, and little John, when he was four and five years old, was watching this being filled up with the embankment of the new Dymock railway. Close at hand, adjoining the station, are the kennels of the Ledbury Hunt, and we have the poet's own recollection how 'once when I was, perhaps, five years old, the fox was hunted into our garden, and those glorious beings in scarlet, as well as the hounds, were all about my lairs, like visitants from paradise'.

This alas, was only 'during my first seven years', for he lost both parents in childhood. He commemorates his mother, who died in 1885, in the poem *C.L.M.*, so powerful and beautiful that it will remain a landmark in English literature, but so poignant and intimate that I do not quote it in this personal narrative. Mrs. Masefield's maiden name was Caroline Louisa Parker, she being the daughter of the rector of Great Comberton, Worcestershire. John Masefield's child-recollection of his mother's beauty expressed in *C.L.M.* is not strained, for a motherly landlady in Ledbury told me, both from her own recollection and her parents' comments, that Mrs. Masefield was a lovely woman.

I must dwell for a moment on this period of emergence from the innocence of childhood, because it might have peculiar significance in the case of one who has that intense insight into character, and power of observation which makes a poet. Such power, if inborn, comes out in infancy. Wordsworth's *Intimations of Immortality* expresses this.

That lately discovered Hereford poet Thomas Traherne, who lived from 1636 to 1674, analyses and describes this in lovely prose in his *Centuries of Meditations*. He points out how:

> The first Light which shined in my Infancy in its primitive and innocent clarity was totally eclipsed insomuch that I was fain to learn all again ... by a whole sea of other matters and concernments that covered and drowned it: finally by the evil influence of a bad education which did not foster and cherish it ... and at last all the celestial, great, and stable treasures to which I was born, as wholly forgotten, as if they had never been.

The amazing fact that Traherne reveals is the extremely early age at which this mental struggle begins in the case of a poet:

> Once I remember (I think I was about four years old) when I thus reasoned with myself, sitting in a little obscure room in my father's poor house; 'If there be a God, certainly he must be infinite in Goodness'; and that I was prompted to by a real whispering instinct of Nature.

It happens that I have first-hand evidence of the early age at which John Masefield's poet-instincts of keen observation and deduction began to assert themselves. I have related in another chapter that in 1881, I journeyed by canoe on the canal past The Knapp, the new railway embankment already advancing to threaten and fill up that part of the canal. John Masefield, watching the progress, was then not three years old, and the whole of the obliteration near Ledbury must have been completed before he was five leaving, it is true, a bit of isolated canal above the town. The completed line was opened to the public in July 1885.

And yet in *The Widow in the Bye Street*, we get detailed observation of this making of the embankment, of the inn which the navvies frequented and of the stores in the station yard, which must have ceased to exist when he was only seven. In a letter to me too (1922) he remarked, 'It was a pity the canal was abandoned, it was a romantic highway to my childhood.' And at the only time I have met John Masefield (October 1930), he said so again.

The Knapp in the Homend, where John Masefield was born

Can it be that the child-mind, at the turn and crisis of his life at seven, successfully rebelled, refused to allow the vision splendid to die away, and fade into the light of common day; a mental rebellion lasting through boyhood, and gaining victory years later?

We, who listened to the simple sincerity and clarity of his Hereford address, felt the child-mind turned to manhood speaking, and a critic in the London daily press made a similar comment. As to external things, he 'heard the whisper of water nigh me', and down the canal with the little Leddon flowing alongside past Hazel Mill, his heart went towards ships and the port of Gloucester.

'My home', says the poet, 'during my first seven years, was within half-a-mile of the Kennels. Later in my childhood, although I lived less near to the Kennels, I was still within about a mile of them and saw hounds frequently, at all seasons.' The change indicated was soon after his mother's death for, the father being very ill, a move was made to The Priory, a large house built by his grandfather, George, beyond the church. At his father's death, a year or two later, the family of six sons and daughters were adopted by their uncle, William Masefield, living at The Priory with his childless wife. I gather that a governess was part of a busy household.

The outdoor lure of streams and water, of woods and the hunt, enlarged the life of the boy. 'I remember Mr. Ballard well', he wrote in the letter to me which I have quoted. 'He had a marvellous ship-model, which I think he had rigged in the rig of 1750 or thereabouts.' And again in *Roadways*, written of his early yearnings:

> One road leads to London,
> One road leads to Wales,
> My road leads me seawards,
> To the white dipping sails.

Days on foot with the Ledbury Hunt came, exercising that intense observation of the countryside which even then began to bear fruit.

Of course 'the romantic boy', as I have heard him called in Ledbury, was different in thought and action from other lads of his class. We can see this, the beginnings of a mental revolt, in sonnets written of childhood at The Knapp, when:

> God lived in a cottage up the brook,
> Beauty, you lifted up my sleeping eyes
> And filled my heart with longing with a look.
> And all the day I searched but could not find
> The beautiful dark-eyed who touched me there.

And then at night, when 'the owls were watching in the yew' (there is a large yew against the house):

> The midnight filled the quiet house with awe.
> So, creeping down the stair, I drew the bolt
> And passed into the darkness, and I knew
> That Beauty was brought near by my revolt.
>
> (*Sonnets*)

It was a home full of the kindliest family sympathies; it is easy to sense that in Ledbury. Here, however, was a small boy different from the others, going off by himself, always watching the 'lower classes', and secretly writing bits of rhyme; playing cricket, the family game, it is true, but not with his whole heart, when his father and uncle before him, and his brothers coming on, so often reached top scores in local and county matches. If any one of us conventional folk – or perhaps rather our sisters and cousins and aunts – had been there, we should not have understood. We know now that it was the childhood of a budding poet laureate, but we should not then have thought of that. Let us keep in mind, too, that his contact with the Ledbury countryside practically ceased soon after he was 14. It was however a boyhood full of happy experiences:

> The gift of country life, near hills and woods,
> Where happy waters sing in solitudes.
>
> (*Biography*)

We are told too, of 'the merry days in the old home before I went to sea'.

John Masefield went to King Edward's School at Warwick. There are many indications in his poems of a boyhood knowledge of Shropshire, and even a preference towards linking himself to that shire. His family came from there; High Ercall is mentioned several times, and he visited and was impressed by the surviving wall at the Roman town of Wroxeter.

After school, his longing for the sea prevailed. He went on H.M. Training Ship *Conway*, and Ledbury people remember him in his uniform. I quote an informed statement from about 1930:

> From there, he went on a voyage as an apprentice round Cape Horn. He was very ill on the voyage and invalided home. He got another appointment and was to have joined his ship in America, but instead chose the life of a rover in the States, and much of his experience during that time appears in his earlier prose books. A few years later, he returned home and obtained an appointment in the Capital and Counties Bank in London, and it was then that he started seriously on his literary career. He found after a time that he could support himself in this way, and gave up his appointment at the Bank.

I give a conversation I had with a Ledbury farmer the other day who (like me) is a score or more years older than the poet. I jotted it down the same day.

> The Masefields – of course I have known all of them – and as upright a family they are as ever stepped. I was looking at Charlie Masefield's little lad going down the street the other day and it turned my mind to their great-grandfather, George. You know he took to an old lawyer's business in Ledbury – was it Holbrook? I fancy that was the name. My father had got some bit of property tangled up in the office somehow, with lawyer's fees totting up on it. George Masefield went very straight and got it all put to rights, without running up bills like the other one had done.
>
> Young John – yes, I remember him – his uncle William, who had no chicks of his own, had brought up all Edward's

children in his own house and once, when I met him in the street, he said to me: 'That lad John settles down to nothing. I don't rightly know what to make of him.' But there, what could you expect?

> Of course he was not built like the others; he could see right through things, whether it was a horse, or a dog, or a man's character, or friends and trees, or things about a farm. And put it all down on paper into the bargain. Nothing but getting away from lawyer's offices and schools would do for his sort. So William saw that he was 'prenticed to the merchant shipping, and we didn't hear of him for a few years.

In my photograph of the Old Talbot Inn, of the time of Masefield's boyhood, two theatre play bills are in the window. The leading line LEAH caught my eye lately, for I was once stage-carpenter and property-man in that play when Miss Bateman 'From the Lyceum Theatre, London' brought it to my father's public hall at Hereford. This bill, however, was for a much humbler affair, strolling players in a wooden booth, which I remember having seasons of several weeks at a time at Hereford, and local towns. They were known as Holloway's Theatre, and acted a different play each night, such as *Leah, The Jewish Maiden*; *Maria Martin*, or *The Murder in the Red Barn*. When they had a pitch at Ledbury, I gather that young John Masefield saw Tom Holloway, their leading man, in *The Land of Gold*, or *The Sea of Ice*, and caught there the first glamour of the boards.

Out in the world
Before coming to the literary records of our countryside to be found in the poet's work, there intervene those 'years blank with hardship' which made him.

He did not become a seaman, for he found his queen-the-sea in her most cruel and relentless mood and got back, bruised and shattered, to the land again. Glimpses of the hard years which followed will be found in his poems, such as *Biography*. A man now in our county told me that when at Yonkers, then a village, now unrecognisable as almost a suburb of New York, he knew the carpet mill where Masefield found work at one time. At Greenwich Village, New York, an inn or saloon where he found work is recorded in a press paragraph. If, in those hard years, the iron entered into the soul of one who was then a mere lad, it all left no resentments or regrets in his work, and we can assure him that it contributed grip and backbone to his artistry.

The Old Talbot Inn.
Note the playbills displayed in the downstairs windows.

Ships, and those who go down to the sea in them, remained as themes of passionate interest and he started as the poet laureate of 'The man with too weighty a burden, too weary a load' before he became the national one. Through it all gleamed the beacon light – afar off – of his artist's goal, and came the setting of teeth and determination that 'it will go on'.

Masefield drifted to the great city. 'London Town of all towns, I'm glad to leave behind', he wrote later, but where else can a writer go to sell his wares? Fortunately he found some helpful literary companionship and got to be known a little. Then commenced his output. First short poems – *Trade Winds* in the *Outlook* of 5th October 1901 and *Cardigan Bay* in that of 23rd November 1901. Next year *The Speaker* took two little poems of his native shire, *On Malvern Hill* and *The West Wind*, with a touch of home-sickness; maybe a special meaning can be read in it.

> It's the white road westward is the road I must tread
> To the green grass, the cool grass, and rest for heart and head,
> To the violets and the warm hearts and the thrushes' song,
> In the fine land, the west land, the land where I belong.

These songs and many others were published in his first book, *Salt-Water Ballads*, November 1902, with its defiant 'consecration' to 'the ranker, the tramp of the road … the drowsy man at the wheel, the tired lookout'. 'Some of this was written in my boyhood, all in my youth', writes Masefield years later; and in it are four recollections of his homeland.

Few poets have ever presented a volume containing so many songs which sing in one's ears at first reading. I am afraid that Masefield has turned from this particular type in later days. Has the very discreditable custom grown up in musical circles of refusing to give credit to the originator of such fine songs anything to do with this? Take such a lyric as *Sea Fever*:

> I must go down to the seas again, to the lonely sea and the sky
> And all I ask is a tall ship and a star to steer her by,

And the wheel's kick and the wind's song and the white sails shaking,
And a grey mist on the sea's face and a grey dawn breaking.

What human message can any tune writer add to this? Does it not contain such an ideal picture and lilt and rhythm, that music can only heighten and add a shade of beauty at the best? At the worst (and I hear this often), music can ruin the poet's conception. The same remark applies to all other writers of great songs. To give a specific instance of an almost invariable custom now, the BBC programme on 18th February 1931 had in sequence *Three Salt-Water Ballads* (from the above book) and *Four Child Songs* (from Stevenson's *A Child's Garden of Verses*) with only the musical setter of the songs given credit by name. Surely it would not strain space much to give the double credit, thus Masefield-Keel and Stevenson-Quilter?

Then, as the next seven years slipped by, other volumes of poems, a few of prose, work on the *Manchester Guardian*, and several novels. These had, as *Captain Margaret*, a quality and a sense of predestination which I have found to encourage a second and third reading.

It is outside the scope of this book to detail the whole range of Masefield's life and very diversified writings. Remember his fine prose, his plays, culminating in the religious series – one, *The Coming of Christ,* to be acted in Canterbury Cathedral. I will mention his earliest, *The Tragedy of Nan,* because the high ambition of its writer is outlined in its introduction, and its action is placed 'among a people, and in a place well known to me'. This is Broad Oak on Severn, which is not in the Cotswold district, as someone has wrongly stated, for it is on the other side of a great tidal river. It was written in 1907, at Greenwich, where Masefield had moved to be near water.

I do not know at what stage of the poet's career his work got to be known in his homeland. I have 'heard tell' in Ledbury how it was Tom Ballard, down on a home-visit, who met old William Masefield, and the talk turned on John's spending time on verse-writing. 'But do you know,' Ballard said, 'that his poems are begin-ning to be talked about and read up in London?' And the other at once said, 'Oh, is that so? Then I must get the book and read them.'

More direct evidence than the above tells me how Masefield's work was attracting attention in Cambridge, by one of supreme judgement. My son, Allen Watkins, was up at Cambridge from 1908 to 1912, a contemporary of Rupert Brooke, whom he knew fairly well. They were talking of poetry one day when Brooke remarked, 'Masefield is the man who is writing good poetry now; you ought to read *Pompey the Great.*' The date of this remark is fixed by *Pompey the Great,* then just out, being issued in April 1910, and *The Everlasting Mercy* (which Allen bought on this advice when it came out in magazine form in October 1911) being not then published.

My son, until then, had only known the name of Masefield in Herefordshire cricket fields, and did not mention the episode until, in 1931, he and I, after a walk over Eastnor Knoll, Deadman's Thorn, Wood Top Field, and down 'the stony wood path to the town', were resting on a seat at Dog Hill, and looking down on the roofs of Ledbury Town, with its near spire dominating the view.

'In London', wrote one who seemed to know, 'he longed for the sight of anything that reminded him of ships and the sea', and after Greenwich, moving to Maida Vale, 'he chose a house overlooking the Regents Canal. Even the sight of the barges served to set memory working again.' The writer of this would not have known, as I do, that the memory was of child-days, glimpses of horse and boat, and statuesque figures drifting slowly past the bottom of his father's garden.

'London has been my prison', he tells us again, and when he escaped it was to the countryside, not to the sea, nor to his home-land, to Berkshire for a time, a lonely farm on Lollington Downs approached only by a rough cart-road; then finally to the Oxford suburb of Boars Hill.

The turning point in Masefield's literary career was when the *English Review* accepted his long narrative poem *The Everlasting*

Mercy, and filled the whole of one number with it. This, in October 1911, was an instantaneous success, and new editions of his previous poems were soon called for.

I must sketch the outline and theme, for the scene is laid in his native town of Ledbury, not however mentioned by name.

The Everlasting Mercy

In his first book Masefield announced his intention of championing the underdog, and selected the seaman, presenting thumb-

View of Ledbury from Dog Hill 1931

nail sketches of sometimes the hardships, sometimes the pleasures (rather brutal and crude ones), and sometimes the romance and beauty of his life. The technique adopted was frankly to use the language of the class even to the verge of offensiveness.

The aim of *The Everlasting Mercy* goes much further. The poet takes the same basis for his literary epic that William Booth was doing in actual social work. It is that which Shakespeare puts in the mouth of Henry the Fifth: 'There is some soul of goodness in things evil, /Would men observingly distil it out.' The technique Masefield adopted is based on the fact that we should not know there was such a quality of goodness if we were not equally aware of evil. That godliness, as a recognised quality, depends on a knowledge of beastliness. And as the theme selected is the emergence of godliness out of beastliness in the real life of a man, the poet depicts the latter quality with somewhat appalling frankness, using actual words and expressions which we all know are part of low-life talk. It is a wholesome frankness, quite free from any veiled gloating on, or glossing over, the evil depicted.

Masefield here goes back to his own countryside and gives us, in the form of a tale in verse, the epic of the conversion to a clean life of a foul-living country-town poacher. The key-note is sincerity.

Saul Kane, depicted as living in a past generation, tells his own vile history:

> From '61 to '67
> I lived in disbelief of Heaven.
> I drunk, I fought, I poached, I whored,
> I did despite unto the Lord,
> I cursed, 'twould make a man look pale,
> And nineteen times I went to gaol.

He quarrelled and had a set fight with another poacher, organised by 'Silas Jones, that bookie wide', keeper of the back-lane inn where the sots meet. There, in an upstairs room, Saul spends his winnings with his pals:

Hot Hollands punch on top of stout
Puts madness in and wisdom out.
From drunken man to drunken man
The drunken madness raged and ran.
'I'm climber Joe who climbed the spire.'
'You're climber Joe the bloody liar.'
'Who says I lie?' 'I do.'
                              'You lie,
I climbed the spire and had a fly.' ...

From three long hours of gin and smokes,
And two girls' breath and fifteen blokes,
A warmish night, and windows shut,
The room stank like a fox's gut.
The heat and smell and drinking deep
Began to stun the gang to sleep.
Some fell downstairs to sleep on the mat,
Some snored it sodden where they sat ...

I opened window wide and leaned
Out of that pigsty of the fiend
And felt a cool wind go like grace
About the sleeping market-place.
The clock struck three, and sweetly, slowly,
The bells chimed Holy, Holy, Holy;
And in a second's pause there fell
The cold note of the chapel bell,
And then a cock crew, flapping wings,
And summat made me think of things.

After each episode in the book, and they follow quickly, some spark of the soul of goodness in Saul makes him 'think of things'.

Stripped of clothes, he madly rings the fire-bell at St. Katherine's near the market-place. He 'shouted fire at doors of parson, lawyer, squire', and smashed their windows. Next day there are other episodes, one being a slanging match across the way by almshouse pump with 'Old parson, red-eyed as a ferret'. Masefield is not partisan in such discussions, and gives both sides. Here is the end of the parson's say:

"Meanwhile, my friend, 'twould be no sin
To mix more water in your gin.
We're neither saints nor Philip Sidneys,
But mortal men with mortal kidneys."
He took his snuff, and wheezed a greeting,
And waddled off to mothers' meeting;
I hung my head upon my chest,
I give old purple parson best.

At night another drinking bout, but:

There used to be a custom then,
Miss Bourne, the Friend, went round at ten ....
She come to us near closing time
When we were at some smutty rhyme.

As a rule, 'None gave her a dirty word', but Saul, 'Mad and ripe for fun', did. The men in the bar grinned. They wondered how Miss Bourne would take it.

"Saul Kane", she said "when next you drink
Do me the gentleness to think
That every drop of drink accursed
Makes Christ within you die of thirst,
That every dirty word you say
Is one more flint upon His way,
Another thorn about His head,
Another mock by where He tread,
Another nail, another cross,
All that you are is that Christ's loss."
The clock run down and struck a chime
And Mrs. Si said, "Closing time."

The wet was pelting on the pane
And something broke inside my brain ...
I got a glimpse of what it meant,
How she and I had stood before
In some old town by some old door,
Waiting intent while someone knocked
Before the door for ever locked ...

[Si's] wife primmed lips and took the till.
Miss Bourne stood still and I stood still,
And "Tick. Slow. Tick. Slow" went the clock.
She said, "He waits until you knock." ...

I heard her clang the Lion door,
I marked a drink-drop roll to floor; ...
A drop from my last glass of gin;
And someone waiting to come in,
A hand upon the door latch gropen
Knocking the man inside to open. …

Out into darkness, out to night,
My flaring heart gave plenty light, …
I did not think, I did not strive,
The deep peace burnt my me alive;
The bolted door had broken in,
I knew that I had done with sin.

Saul Kane wanders down the Homend in wild wind and rain in his state of ecstasy:

The station brook, to my new eyes,
Was babbling out of Paradise;
The waters rushing from the rain
Were singing Christ has risen again.

One can only here give the merest outline of the lovely ending to the epic. The many local touches:

The narrow station-wall's brick ledge,
The wild hop withering in the hedge,
The lights in huntsman's upper storey
Were parts of an eternal glory,
Were God's eternal garden flowers.
I stood in bliss at this for hours.

O glory of the lighted soul.
The dawn came up on Bradlow Knoll ....

"It's dawn", I said, "and chimney's smoking,
And all the blessed fields are soaking.

It's dawn, and there's an engine shunting;
And hounds, for huntsman's going hunting.
It's dawn and I must wander north
Along the road Christ led me forth."

So up the road I wander slow
Past where the snowdrops used to grow
With celandines in early springs,
When rainbows were triumphant things
And dew so bright and flowers so glad,
Eternal joy to lass and lad.

What a tender memory this of the poet's own childhood, wandering down the road with his little sister, for it is all within a few fields of their first home.

And past the lovely brook I paced,
The brook whose source I never traced,
The brook, the one of two which rise
In my green dream in Paradise ...
A gipsy's camp was in the copse,
Three felted tents, with beehive tops, …

A cup of tea at the hawkers' van

Ledbury Park from the Southend with caravans in front

These are the poorer type, and there follows a whimsical comment on the unalterable wandering habits of the race. They stream through Ledbury just after hop-picking, and I show some of their better type caravans waiting under the squire's house [Ledbury Park] while the men are drinking at an inn. Home then across the fields, along the brook, 'past the trap made for the mill', then through a gate into Callows Lane, which is Plaistow Lane.

Here he met with the fruition of 'The Everlasting Mercy'. He had seen 'from Bullen Bank, on Gloucester road', as many Ledbury folk had done from Dog Hill for generations, in the clump of Scotch Firs on the summit of the ten-mile distant May Hill, showing in its suggestive outline, silhouetted against the sky:

> The ploughman patient on the hill
> Forever there, forever still,
> Ploughing the hill with steady yoke
> Of pine-trees lightning-struck and broke.

To Saul Kane now comes the sound of 'a ploughman's voice, a clink of chain':

> Old Callow, stooped above the hales,
> Ploughing the stubble into wales.
> His grave eyes looking straight ahead,
> Shearing a long straight furrow red; …
>
> Slow up the hill the plough team plod,
> Old Callow at the task of God.

There in the bare earth, the poacher's new-cleansed mind sees his task:

> I knew that Christ was there with Callow,
> That Christ was standing there with me,
> That Christ had taught me what to be,
> That I should plough, and as I ploughed
> My Saviour Christ would sing aloud.

The topographical references to the little town in the poem are faithfully exact – up to a point, one well known to writers: that where some slur might fall on living persons.

The scene of the fight, south of the Worcester Road, up beyond the top of the Biddulph deer park, on Wood Top Field where the golf links now are, is clear. So, too, the short cut, between the walls of Cabbage Walk, when returning to the town, where next day Kane, 'made a haul' of 'two ripe pears from lawyer's wall', and one can still see the pear tree over the garden wall of those old-world premises (called The Cloisters), which three generations of Masefields have occupied as offices. Then through the churchyard, past a stone under the yew-tree where:

> The carved heads on the church looked down
> On "Russell, Blacksmith of this Town".

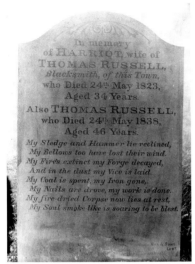

Tomb of Thomas Russell and his wife Harriet, Ledbury churchyard

Note here the accurate memory of the poet, writing at a distance, remembering the two words which were unusually provided on the stone with capitals.

The rowdy troop passed through the churchyard gates, and 'all went quiet down the Scallenge' – the bit of open space between the Reader's House at the top of Church Street and the Police Court. The route down Church Lane, where Mutlow's tannery then was, and where 'The houses put their heads together' is unmistakable. Then comes a bit of purposeful confusion, for the writer does not intend the reader to identify his disreputable drunkard's inn with any still in business and, therefore, (in my opinion) indicates a false site and describes a mixture of several of the smaller Ledbury inns. It is stated that 'at the turning/ The Lion had a window burning' ; this turning must be where Church Lane enters the Market-Place but, from my own observation, I know that at no time in the past half-century has there been an inn whose site could be so described.

Quite five years before John Masefield was to Ledbury people 'a chiel amang you takin' notes', I knew well the inside of all these back-street inns and their landlords, almost all of them kindly and decent folk, as I was going to them to sell the very stout (from my father's brewery) named in the tale. It is the worst of night tavern-life there depicted, not the average, and it must be kept in mind that it was sketched as in a past generation. But I know that it is a true picture.

At the first talk I gave on Masefield, some ten years ago, a man came to me at the end and said, 'I was living in Ledbury when a drunkard broke out of Sam Bowler's at the White Hart and ran, quite naked, to climb the steeple. It was not he, but another, who ran a-muck after pulling the fire-bell.'

That language in a country town is still 'frequent and free' I noted when passing the end of the Bye Street a few months ago. I heard, in the fifteen seconds occupied in walking past two groups of youths on the pavement, the word 'bloody' spoken four times. At this rate it might well be used a thousand times to the hour in the Market-Place. No wonder the soil of Herefordshire is red! But after all, the word only means 'very' in the vulgar tongue.

Most of the inns brewed their own ordinary ale in those early days, and bought 'stout' and 'bitter'. Only the other day I came on an old ex-innkeeper of my acquaintance in a disused brew-house in the Church Lane, and secured for our museum an old style bailing-pail used in the home-brewing days. A bright, clean-faced, blue-eyed little old man he is, and certainly was never a Silas Jones. But he was the chief bookie of the town when he kept the adjoining inn, and is now the mainstay of a nearby church. Folk say that it was a case of sudden conversion.

In the old days he always boasted that he would never drink his own brewed beer; but in contrast, the innkeeper at the Brewery Inn always boasted that he never drank anything but his own brew.

The characters in *The Everlasting Mercy* are composite; several went to make up Saul Kane. One still hears of Great G–, the poacher who stopped at nothing: how that, out with a companion at the top of the squire's park, he said 'Shall I get some venison?', was over the tall palings of perhaps the only deer-park in England which comes right down to the streets of a town, and in ten minutes was back throwing over the fence the carcass of a plump roe which was then and there cut up, carried down to town, and not a sign left on the ground.

Saul Kane himself is a recognisable character, and those who look at my photograph of the man with a gun looking over a hedge, the evening sun in his eyes, can judge whether I did not catch the type. It was many years before the book was written

The Poacher

and many miles from Ledbury that I made my study of 'The Poacher'.

Then the type of 'Old Callow, at the task of God'. Where had I seen 'his grave eyes looking straight ahead'? They are the eyes of the plough-bred man fixed on distant furrow or cop-stick to secure that splendid straightness. My mind went back to a farmer near Ledbury from whom I used to buy wheat to grind in my mill, who had this steady gaze. Not that old farmer Callow was a real man, his name being obviously taken from Callow Hills Farm two miles out of Ledbury.

There is a touch of poetry still in the idea of a miller's trade, and it is expressed in the official motto of the National Association of British and Irish Millers, with its old form alliteration as used in *Piers Plowman*:

The golden grain, God's gift we grind

The Callow Lane is really Plaistow Lane, that short cut past the Rea Farm which, before getting out to the Bosbury Road, passes Anna's cottage [home of *The Widow of the Bye Street*].

There is much apparent crudeness in the verse and wording of this epic which is, in the main, intentional, as it is all put into the mouth of a crude uneducated man.

It seems desirable at this stage to touch on a point hinted at in the opening of the chapter. We all know the type of tale-monger who has confidential information about the private life of public men: 'I can assure you my dear that it is a fact, because I had it from a lady whose cousin was …'. Or : 'I ask you, as a man of the world, is it likely that a young fellow who …'.

It happens that the framework of John Masefield's early life lends itself to this sort of tale, which often becomes a consolidated lie impossible to overtake. For he went to sea very early, led a roving and adventurous life, and wrote with great frankness on low life. Let me grasp this nettle. The phrase 'He ran away to sea' cannot be applicable to one who had training on *The Conway*, and was apprenticed on a ship by his uncle.

I have been in and out of his birth-town when he was rising to fame, and long before and after, and naturally have talked with townsfolk about him. Two facts emerge: all speak with the utmost respect of the lad; and not one, (and I know those who had opportunities of judging), gave the slightest hint of Masefield having taken any part in the life he depicts in this book. 'Had he been not gentle we should know more of him.'

The Widow in the Bye Street

Next year, 1912, another low-life story in verse, the scene again laid in Ledbury, came out. It is likely that the awkwardness, if not impossibility, of getting the word 'Herefordshire' into smooth running verse is the reason why Masefield, beginning thus: 'Down Bye Street in a little Shropshire Town', kept up the illusion, repeated several times, that widow Gurney really did live in Shropshire.

The story is of a decent lad, his mother's support, led by a worthless strumpet into jealousy and murder. It is a tragedy, written with the same frank treatment of the animal side of a poor man's life as the previous book.

Young Jim Gurney worked as a navvy on the making of the new line in the old canal bed, as described on page 88. There is no mistaking the little inn where the lad drank himself into a murder frenzy. It is there, near the station, but without the former licence:

> An inn so hidden it is out of sight
> To anyone not coming from the west,
> The high embankment hides it with its crest …
> Canal men used it when the barges came,
> The navvies used it when the line was making.

Then, Plaisters End, the scene of the murder, has its position exactly described by the short cut across the fields taken from the inn, and the longer way 'by the mills' followed by the old mother. Plaistow is the name for the hamlet on the map. But the house which I see as 'Anna's cottage at the bend', with its half-acre and hen-run, is just below and called Storesbrook.

Finally, when 'Singing her crazy song the mother goes', down below the bridge at the bottom of the Bye Street, beauty is again contrasted with piteous tragedy:

> And in the sunny dawns of hot Julys,
> The labourers going to meadow see her there
> Rubbing the sleep out of their heavy eyes,
> They lean upon the parapet to stare;
> They see her plaiting basil in her hair
> Her singing lingers with them as they mow,
> And many times they try it, now grave, now gay,
> Till, with full throat, over the hills away
> They lift it clear; oh, very clear it towers
> Mixed with the swish of many falling flowers.

The Express Inn, colloquially known as the Bull and Boar on the Hereford Road under the railway embankment. It closed shortly after 1910.

The widow 'gazing from her door', as seen by Alfred Watkins

It is not in her last tragic phase, nor in the Bye Street, but in another back-lane of Ledbury, that I found, years before the book was written, my illustration of the widow gazing from her door 'For Jemmy coming from work along the line'.

Dauber

This fine sea-epic, about the same length as the two preceding poems, came out in 1912. Beauty is again contrasted with tragedy and one cannot help feeling that the dogged determination to pursue his art (drawing in this case) by the country-bred lad at sea, expressed in his dying words as he crashed to death from the riggings: 'It will go on', is in some degree a bit of autobiography.

The description of Dauber's boyhood in Pauntley (which is in the Ledbury hunt district) brings the story into this record, and it may be that it also contains other enlightening touches as regards the poet's own early cravings. The sea passages in the book will live in literature.

The Daffodil Fields

The last of the series of four tales in verse, it was published in 1913. The site is about a mile and a half out of Ledbury in the Hall House meadows, not far from the Gloucester road, and at the Ledbury edge of the well known stretch of daffodil country on the Dymock side. Here again, for some artistic reason, it is named as in Shropshire.

Reynard the Fox

One more book only of Masefield's I note, to throw a light upon our Herefordshire countryside. And what a bible of English pre-war open-air life it is; that phase of life continued without check from the time when, on the same ground, the British race had to hunt of necessity for food. A joyous galloping epic of a day with the hounds. Not a word wasted from the opening line: 'The meet was at the Cock and Pye' to the finish, when the tired men and hounds of the hunt are at rest in those kennels which the poet had adored in his childhood – to the end when from nearby Ledbury Town 'A clock struck twelve and the church-bells chimed'.

It is in two parts, the second one written from the hunted fox's point of view, for here as usual Masefield takes no sides in differences of opinion; enough it is to record facts faithfully. And what a record this is – no small detail omitted. Here, for instance, the stable-men's preparations:

> A pad-groom gave a cloth a beating,
> Knocking the dust out with a stake.
> Two men cleaned stalls with fork and rake,
> And one went whistling to the pump,
> The handle whined, ker-lump, ker-lump.
> The water splashed into the pail,
> And, as he went, it left a trail,
> Lipped over on the yard's bricked paving.

Masefield mentions the aim of this book in his article *Fox Hunting*, that it 'gave an opportunity for a picture or pictures of the members of an English community ... The whole of the land's society brought together, focussed for the observer, as the Canterbury Pilgrims were for Chaucer.' Is not his slim volume the best thing of the kind since Chaucer? His character-sketches probing to the very soul. Some, of thumb-nail length:

> Carlotta Ilsley brought her love,
> A flop-jowled broker from the city.
> Men pitied her, for she was pretty.

Others, half-sheet-of-note-paper length:

> Pete Gurney was a lusty cock
> Turned sixty-three, but bright and hale,
> A dairy-farmer in the vale,

> Much like a robin in the face,
> Much character in little space,
> With little eyes like burning coal;
> His mouth was like a slit or hole
> In leather that was seamed and lined.
> He had the russet-apple mind
> That betters as the weather worsen.
> He was a manly English person,
> Kind to the core, brave, merry, true.

One would like to give full samples of these 85 sketches, men and women of every contrasting type. Sal Ridden, daughter of Tom See, the trainer:

> A loud, bold, blonde, abundant mare
> With white horse-teeth and stooks of hair.

Contrasted with her, her daughter Belle:

> A strange, shy, lovely girl, whose face
> Was sweet with thought and proud with race,
> And bright with joy at riding there.

Farmer Bennett, on his big-boned savage black, as grim as his steed:

> He'd given many a man a lathering
> In field or barn, and women too.
> His cold eye reached the women through
> With comment, and the men with scorn.
> He hated women gently born.

Charles Copse, loved through the countryside:

> No heart of youth could ever doubt him
> Or fail to follow where he led.
> He was a genius, simply bred.

The poet let himself go on the hounds, as Shakespeare did, and gives three pages to their engaging manners:

> Those feathery things, the hounds, in front.
> Intent, wise, dipping, trotting, straying,

Smiling at people, shoving, playing,
Nosing to children's faces, waving
Their feathery sterns, and all behaving.

How Masefield revels in the country place-names, pieced-up by him from bits of Herefordshire, Gloucestershire and Berkshire names. Here is the fox's run to find a vixen:

By Tencombe Regis and Slaughters Court,
Through the great grass square of Roman Fort,
By Nun's Wood Yews and the Hungry Hill,
And the Corpse Way Stones all standing still.
By Seven Springs Mead to Deerlip Brook,
And a lolloping leap to Water Hook.

I must not even sketch the run. It was Dansey the whip and Dawe the huntsman who saw the last of it, when:

And the hunt came home and the hounds were fed,
They climbed to their bench and went to bed;
The horses in stable loved their straw.
"Good-night, my beauties," said Robin Dawe.

John Masefield, in his *Fox Hunting* preface, explains the localities in his mind for the run:

These real and imaginary fields, woods and brooks are taken, as they exist, from Berkshire, where the fox lives, from Herefordshire, where he was found, from Trapalanda, Gloucestershire, Buckinghamshire, Herefordshire, Worcestershire and Berkshire, where he ran, from Trapalanda, where he nearly died, and from a wild and beautiful corner in Berkshire where he rests from his run.

To some of us, this very wide range seems the one blemish in the topic, for the Downs country, with its chalk and flint, is not coherent with (or near to) our 'old red', hill-coppices and deep clay'. But the poet tells us how, as a boy, he 'went to many meets, and followed many hunts on foot' and then got his experiences, for 'I was much in the woods as a boy'.

An acquaintance of years ago (Mr. C.N. Carter, who spent his boyhood at Cradley about that time, or a year or two earlier) tells me in a letter that in those days the Ledbury Hunt met as follows:

Monday on the Dymock, Newent and Aston Ingham side. Wednesday on the Cradley and Bosbury side. Friday on the 'Duke of York' and Tewkesbury side. Saturday on the Ledbury, Eastnor and British Camp side.

Mr. Carter, who used to see either John Masefield or his brother at these meets, adds:

We were always taught that with wild animals the essential thing was to be quiet, and therefore my brothers and I generally kept very much to ourselves, and did not encourage talking when we were hunting. We did however make an exception of the real natives, and generally had a chat with the farmers and labourers, with whom we never had a wrong word. I never remember being ordered off ... Of all the spots in the Ledbury Hunt Country, the stand I used to take close to Walm's Well was the one I was fondest of, and I think that I viewed more foxes there than in any other part of the hunt.

Walm's Well – on the ridge footpath between Herefordshire Beacon and Midsummer Hill, near Clutter's Cave

Reynard the Fox, an epic which must become a classic, was certainly born in this countryside west and south of the Malverns, and many of us recognise fragments of real characters, real places, and real names of the district, all chopped up, mixed, and reunited (as in mince-meat) to a convincing reality. Often a place-name is converted to a personal one, and vice-versa. In the preface the name 'Heydigate' is a place, but Heygate is the name of a Herefordshire hunting family.

Many of the personal names are to be found as names in the Berkshire map. Both Herefordshire and Berkshire people will pick out half-a-dozen characters from the 85 depicted and say 'I recognise that as so and so', while readers up in the north, where Masefield has not lived, would not do so. But this is simply a tribute to the creative craftsmanship of the poet, for each character is an imaginary one, built up out of the common stock of the writer's impressions of many people he has seen, and the names from fleeting recollections of real names he has once read.

Sometimes, a place-name is a real one, or very near it. 'The Boyce' is the local name for Boyce Court, a hunting-squire's home on the canal near Dymock, and Clench Brook Mill is on the map near Ledbury as Clencher's Mill. At a Ledbury market-dinner long ago I have found the chair taken by a courteous old fox-hunting farmer, always affectionately addressed as 'Squire Harrington', his name, but not his manners, suggesting to me the bitter, stupid 'Squire Harringdew' of Masefield. It is in fact impossible to create quite new names.

The only mention of Ledbury I have seen in Masefield's works is in *The Campden Wonder,* his eighteenth-century Cotswold tragedy, there brought into a contemptuous attack: 'That's what you are – and a dog – a dirty twelve shilling sneck up of a Ledbury lawyer'. This of course applied to lawyers of long ago, and was probably an example of that phase of English humour which relates something against one's own clan. For example, when I had recently given an illustrated lecturette on old world mills and milling (my own trade), the mill foreman sent me the following epitaph which he had copied from Kington Churchyard:

IN MEMORY OF
William Payton
Harpton Mill
In Parish Old Radnor.
A tender Father
A good husband
A sincere Friend
And Honest Man tho'
A Miller

There is a link with the countryside which appears occasionally in John Masefield's work; an insight into the life of prehistoric man on the land. A poet's faculty as a seer and intensely keen observer fits him well for this branch of archaeology, but few of them, save Scott, have followed it up. It comes first as intuition, and accurate observation follows. In front of his child-home the prehistoric camp, Wall Hills, was in full sight. One wonders whether he saw that no stone walls were there, only earthen banks, and pondered on the name: or why a trench on the further side is still the King's Ditch? Certain it is that in later days looking on the 'red brick chinks' of 'old Roman ruins white with pinks' the poet 'felt the hillside thronged by souls unseen, who knew the interest in me, and were keen that man alive should understand man dead'.

Certain it is that he noted on Badon Hill (in connection with the trackway up), that it was 'notched on the skyline by its rampart still', when expert archaeologists, even when they found a paved causeway in (not across) a ditch or rampart, had not followed up the fact. Then again that spot at The Haunted Gate – 'Evil was there, men never went there late.' But someone digging found a hoard of coins:

> So that one knew how, centuries before,
> Some Roman flying from the sack by night
> Digging in terror there to hide his store,
> Sweating his pick, by windy lantern light,
> Had stamped his anguish on that place's soul
> So that it knew and could rehearse the whole.
>
> *(Sonnets)*

A very real thing is this sense of old, old, human occupation on certain spots, and Masefield again brings it out in his masterpiece *August 1914*:

> If there be any life beyond the grave,
> It must be near the men and things we love,
> Some power of quick suggestion how to save,
> Touching the living soul as from above ...
> An influence from the Earth from those dead hearts ...
> A muttering from beyond the veils of Death.

One striking link exists between Masefield and Langland. The plough, that emblem which as a star-group 'tips round the pole', is the goal, the instrument and the background of both poets in their most striking work. It is the test, and the ultimate work-refuge in their ideals. One wonders whether the sign 'in pine-trees lightning struck and broke' which marked the 'May Hill ploughman', goes back to a time when Will Langland could have seen it, for it certainly has survived the adding of new trees in the Jubilee year.

A feature is the intimate working knowledge of the plough shown by the later poet. The plough-foot was originally shaped like a hockey-stick, and was fixed vertically before the coulter (the front cutting knife edge), to slide on the ground and decide how deep the point of the share (the broad blade which slices the earth and turns it over) [would go]. The plough-foot is adjustable up or down; it is hardly known by that name now, as it has become a wheel, with no resemblance to the original foot. But Masefield, like Langland, knows all about its real working:

> His plough-foot high to give it earth
> To bring new food for men to birth.

All poets are seers and even prophets in varying degrees. Langland's vision was political; Masefield has in the main avoided even social politics. But his work is not ended, and there have been indications of a change, commencing with that declaration, the first public one since his award of the laurel wreath, mentioned here as my inspiration. It seems as if his plea may be: 'Back to the Land to toil, to produce, to learn, to build up a better nation.'

The seer and the teacher spoke at the end of his luncheon speech at Hereford in October 1930. He said:

> Here in this county is almost the last stronghold of the old England that was so noble and so wonderful a hundred years ago, which got its living out of the soil. Nations, like individuals, sometimes take after false gods, and false advisors, and make a mess of things. For the last hundred years we have been making a mess of things, following after false gods and devastating our lovely land, which has not made us happy or wealthy. We are poor and seeing the error of our ways, and I hope that in the next generation some saner way of life will be found, so that this land will again get its living and its inspiration out of the soil, and its joys from living near the soil, in kinship with its beauty, which has been so largely threatened and so largely desecrated.

6

The Soul of the Soil

All the earth of England is consecrated by intense memories of the English ... It is one of Shakespeare's humanities that the English country, which made him, always meant much to him, so that now, wherever his works go, something of the soul of that country goes too.

John Masefield

The soul of the soil is something – I know not what – which mother-earth passes into the man who comes into direct contact with her if he finds her clothed only with nature products. A something cut off by metalled or tarred roads, stone or rubber pavements; shut off by roofs or walls, and the town dweller – so long as he keeps in town – knows it not.

This soul is a vitamin essential to the full mental life of man, and the peoples who are starved of it are starved indeed. It varies in degree and quality with the different natures of the soil and the countryside. It is shut out – as is our capacity to imbibe it – by the reek of gas or petrol, or foul chimney fumes.

We blindly express this by a wholesome but only partial craving. The tramp who leaves the road for field tracks feels this, the camper-out, the hiker or field rambler, even the builder of a weekend bungalow. It is three-parts of the joy of the fox-hunter, the fisher, the coursing man, the out-door sportsman of most sorts, including the hare-and-hounds schoolboy, until other attributes of 'sport' obscure or destroy it. The city clergyman who organises his Country Holidays for Children Fund feels well the call of the soil, and its soul.

The gardener, the ploughman, with those who cultivate and drag out the fruits of the soil from the earth, are most of all in touch with and understand its soul, as are those who tend the animals reared on the land. Only partially the gipsy, for he too often gives himself up to the task of outwitting his fellow man, and is not a producer on the earth. The farmer is fundamentally in touch, and is often entirely so, but there are some cases where huckster and bargaining methods become so overwhelmingly his main habit that the other aspect is submerged.

The Romans brought to Britain a clear idea of this soul or spirit, for on an altar found near Glasgow was inscribed 'GENIO TERRAE BRITANNICAE' – 'To the spirit of the British Countryside'. On another Roman altar from near the Wall of Antoninus – 'To the Gods of Britain, from whose fields our food comes'.

There comes the question – does this soul or spirit contribute something to the mentality of those in touch with it? It seems that it does, and here are two indications. In my own experience of manufacturing industries (brewing, milling, instrument-making) it is a fact that the most valuable mechanics and craftsmen are those who came from the land (the country artisan class). Being imbued with the use and repair of all tools and implements used on mother-earth, they have adaptable minds capable of training to any mechanical work and beat the town-bred men in ultimate usefulness.

In one agricultural county where a large motor-factory was founded, many skilled agricultural workers were attracted by the higher wages. Although soon efficient at their repetitive machine job, they could not endure (so reported a speaker on the wireless) the monotony of one repeated and mindless action, and went back to lower wages and the varied skilled jobs which exercise human effort and mind on the farm. But the lads [young and unskilled] going straight from the land to 'the works' did stick it.

The second instance relates more to the higher or intellectual life, and was brought out by a professional dramatic critic reviewing, in a Sunday paper, a play which he described as particularly silly and foolish, and remarked that it seemed suitable for an audience in a small provincial town. The next week appeared a letter asking the critic whether he would kindly indicate the size of the type of town to which he referred. Would it be as small as the village of 'Thrums', where Sir James Barrie was born and trained? Or the small town of Brecon, where Mrs. Siddons was born and had much of her early stage training, or the larger place, Hereford, where David Garrick was born, and William Powell – who almost out-rivalled Garrick in popularity at Drury Lane but died young – also Roger Kemble the strolling player and actor, who trained his daughter, Mrs. Siddons, and three sons, John Phillip, Stephen and Charles, to take high places on the stage, even of London – the great market, but not in the main the great source of dramatic talent? Was the place in the critic's mind a village like the small one in Somersetshire where Henry Irving, 'who came of a yeoman stock', was born; or would it be a small market town like Ledbury where John Masefield was reared? Perhaps (the letter concluded),

Stratford-on-Avon would fit the critic's idea of a pattern for the size of place where a silly play would be best appreciated.

The saying that 'you cannot find three generations of pure-bred Londoners' may not be accurate, but an important truth lies in it, for most of those who make a mark in London are country-bred. The soul of the soil is necessary to rejuvenate our national life, and we confusedly acknowledge this in our phrase 'back to the land'.

I have heard Ramsay MacDonald, speaking on a non-political platform, tell how he was brought up as a working farm-boy in Scotland, and he brought some of the soul of the soil to his office of Prime Minister.

Until now – but the industrial revolution of 150 years ago has imperilled the fact – the very life of Britain has been constantly replenished by a flow into town, or into industrial life, of men and women brought up on the soil. Is not this becoming exhausted?

In 1769 a Fleet Street hack journalist, poet and prophet or seer, saw clearly the danger, and wrote *The Deserted Village* to point it out. But in order that his book might sell he embellished it with descriptive poetic imagery of country life so entrancing that neither his nor following generations have even noticed that the book is the earnest warning cry of a bard or prophet. Dr. Oliver Goldsmith, who came from the Irish countryside, makes it clear in his dedication to Sir Joshua Reynolds that he was intensely in earnest:

> I know that you will object that the depopulation it deplores is nowhere to be seen, and the disorder it laments are only to be found in the poet's imagination. To this I can scarcely make any other answer than that I sincerely believe what I have written; that I have taken all possible pains, in my country excursions, for these four or five years past, to be certain of what I allege.

The warning is well embodied in the poem:

> Ill fares the land, to hastening ills a prey,
> Where wealth accumulates, and men decay:
> Princes and lords may flourish, or may fade;

A breath can make them, as a breath has made;
But a bold peasantry, their country's pride,
When once destroyed can never be supplied. ...

A time there was, ere England's griefs began,
When every rood of ground maintained its man;
For him light Labour spread her wholesome store,
Just gave what life required, but gave no more:
His best companions, Innocence and Health;
And his best riches, ignorance of wealth.

But times are altered; Trade's unfeeling train
Usurp the land, and dispossess the swain ...

Ye friends to truth, ye statesmen who survey
The rich man's joys increase, the poor's decay,
'Tis yours to judge how wide the limits stand
Between a splendid and a happy land. ...
                    ... The man of wealth and pride
Takes up a space that many poor supplied;
Space for his lake, his park's extended bounds;
Space for his horses, equipage and hounds; ...
... His seat, where solitary sports are seen,
Indignant spurns the cottage from the green; ...

Where then, ah! where, shall Poverty reside,
To 'scape the pressure of contiguous Pride?
If to some common's fenceless limits strayed,
He drives his flock to pick the scanty blade,
Those fenceless fields the sons of wealth divide,
And even the bare-worn common is denied.
If to the city sped – What waits him there?
To see profusion that he must not share;
To see ten thousand baneful arts combined
To pamper luxury, and thin mankind. ...

Even now, methinks, as pondering here I stand,
I see the rural Virtues leave the land.
Down where yon anchoring vessel spreads the sail,

That idly waiting flaps with every gale,
Downward they move, a melancholy band,
Pass from the shore, and darken all the strand.

We, who seem to be at the point of exhaustion of the industrial revolution movement, now uneasily feel danger in the air. But I must not turn this book to treatment of our economic problem, even if I could lay down a remedy, which I cannot do.

Two instances of 'the man who knows' springing from the soil may be worth noting:

I had many times, in passing a point where an old hollow road came down to the main road, resolved at some future time to get out and investigate this track. So, passing again one day, I called to my driver to stop the car, but not until it had shot more than a hundred yards beyond the point, so getting out I had to walk back to the junction. Opposite this is a farmhouse, and as I walked along the road centre there came out to meet me a farmer (I did not know him), who as soon as we met face to face said, 'So you've come to see the old road?' I asked in surprise whether he knew who I was, the reply being 'No!' As was also the answer to an enquiry whether he knew that someone was investigating the old tracks. But he added, 'I always know exactly what anyone who comes has called about.' And he proceeded to give some convincing instances of this queer insight. I then put a curious question – 'Are you by chance a bone-setter?' The reply was that as a lad he found he had that faculty with animals, and had often practised it, but not on humans.

This brings up the second instance. A year ago, just over the borders of Herefordshire, near Knighton, the people got up a subscription – not inspired by the clergy or upper classes, although they cordially joined in the movement – as testimony to a local farmer, a member of a traditional bone-setting family, the Lloyds. This amounted to about £400, a token of gratitude for real and often unpaid services in relieving human suffering and crippling conditions. Such insight seems to spring from the soil – a sister of this man, who married a small Herefordshire farmer, found late in life that she possessed the power, and now practises it.

Occasionally the old country tendency for ballad writing crops up, as in the case of a young farmer close under the Black Mountains, using keenly his observation faculties, and then describing all he has noted in a jingle resembling the old traditional ballad form inherited from his forebears. It concerns the road-side chapel he attends. Note his naïve observation of the building, for whose restoration 'these lines I've penned':

> The seats and rostrum are painted oak,
> The walls inside are coloured pink,
> And when we all in praise unite,
> We see the top is painted white.

The spirit of the soil comes out in the broadsheet ballads which I remember being sung and sold in the streets at Hereford May Fair. Such ballads I have heard sung by the fireside in a monotonous treble by a farmer. Whilst staying at another farm, old Jane, who lived in a lone cottage up under a wood, had come down in the evening out of curiosity to see an unusual visitor, and as the farmer's wife had spoken of her memory for old songs and tales, some questions put to her fortunately mentioned an old ballad, with the local name of 'Lord Bateman'. Fortunately, because after some hesitation the old lady recited, not sung, 'The Loving Ballad of Lord Bateman' at full length with creditable dramatic emphasis.

The ploughman, with whose craft both Langland and Masefield are so closely in touch, is saturated with the spirit of the soil. The hedger and ditcher I once photographed, with an over-garment fashioned from a corn sack, is certain to have been at the plough when younger, perhaps even now. He exemplified the worker-on-the-land's knack of making quaint but telling comparisons in his remark, when he noticed awkward trails of thorny briar entangled in the camera legs: 'Take care, sir, they be very loving.' The comparison of this with a sweetheart's arms round your neck would not occur to a town man.

I was sitting in a beer-house on a common near here (closed years ago, I am afraid, for transgressing the licensing laws) and the landlady, having got wind somehow that I had an interest in the brewery from which she bought, began to talk for my benefit.

> You see how it is when the times are so bad, many's the time when Joe and I goes without our bit of meat for dinner, so as the old man may have a bite. That there outride of Watkins's (an 'outride' is a brewer's traveller, which job I had given up years earlier), is very decent, and often leaves me a shilling and it comes in useful, I tells ye.

This a broad hint for me, an unsuspecting caller for a glass of beer. But there comes a very slowly uttered dictum from a quiet man in a corner, 'Well, Mrs. Weaver, them as owns bricks an' mart'r didn't have no need to talk on not hav'n enough ter eat.' (This a reference to the freehold belonging to the landlady.) The waspish reply came quick as a flash: 'Ye can't eat bricks an' mart'r, can ye?'

One more old-time worker on the soil who drags out its essence was old Thomas Map, my father's gardener. He must have sprung from the same stock as Walter Map, the Herefordshire cleric, and was full of landlore. 'Ye may bring your maps of these here fields to look on as long as ye like, but here's a Map as'll tell ye a sight more 'bout 'em than they will.' He liked to talk of the large families of old times. 'There wus a biggish lot of us at home, my feyther had seventeen on us, but then his maister had more, there wur nineteen on 'em. An' one time he axed all on us to dinner, so with the fower feythers an' mothers there were farty on us sat a-table.'

That these quiver-full families are not entirely of long ago in this district is proved by the case of Zachariah Watkins, farmer of Brinsop, (I cannot claim a kinship), who in November 1919 was followed to the grave by twenty of his children, twelve boys and eight girls, who left another sister ill at home. Five of the lads served in the Great War, and all came back. Zachariah married twice, and there seems as much difficulty in counting the total number in his family as there is in counting the yew trees in Painswick churchyard, as one or two more died in infancy, but the total numbers alive at one time seems to have been twenty-two.

Matter more to the point is scattered through Masefield's brilliant short study of Shakespeare, where in the first place that genius is made 'to tell his love for the earth of England, which had ministered to his mind with beauty through his years of youth'. Then, 'the earth of England is a good earth and bears good fruit, even the apple of men'. Also, as regards upper society, 'country society alters very little, it is the enduring stem on which the cities graft fashions'.

Speaking of the type of man produced by the soul of the soil in England brings to mind this comment, to be taken to heart by those who think the stage presentation of a countryman to be 'true to life': 'That beautiful kindness, high courage, and devoted service should go so often with real animal boorishness and the incapacity to see more than one thing at a time (mistaken for stupidity by stupid people), puzzled Shakespeare, as it puzzles the un-English mind to-day.'

It is the town-bred man of the third generation who has to be bucked up by full-page-suggestion-in-'Daily Puffer', to purchase in tablet form enough power of concentration and expert observation on his one subject to be efficient. The country-bred man is already trained.

Truly it is this power to concentrate on one thing at a time, combined with the twin habit of acute observation, which is the valuable gift bestowed by the soul of the soil on man.

Millstone dressing in 1914

Photographers at work at the Dipping Well at Whitchurch, Symonds Yat

Photographs of Herefordshire

by Alfred Watkins

with an introduction by Ron & Jennifer Shoesmith

The gateway to Wigmore Abbey

Alfred Watkins, the photographer

by Ron & Jennifer Shoesmith

In this age of the fully automatic camera, when all the user needs to do is point his pocket-sized machine at the subject and press a button, the complexities and difficulties which had to be overcome to take a successful photograph during the second half of the 19th century tend to be forgotten. Alfred Watkins remembered this in the introduction to his book *Photography: its Principles and Applications*, written in 1911, when he described an outing during 1876, when he was about 21 years old:

> I write this in a Radnorshire roadside inn; the landlady comes in with the bedroom candle; and I bring to mind the day thirty-five years ago when I first came to the inn. It was on a business-driving journey, and in the trap was my wet plate photographic kit. What a proceeding it was in those days; the pitching of the portable tent, sitting on one's heels inside, drawing the flaps, coating the plate with collodion, dipping it in the silver bath to sensitise, carrying out to expose, not far away, for it must be developed while still wet, again cramped, within the low tent. And yet with all the obstacles difficult subjects were attempted.
>
> Over the other side of that great mountain mass – the Radnor Forest – I remember turning out one cold winter's morning and taking scenes on the little frozen stream with the trees hung with hoar frost, and a lighted spirit lamp required in the tent to thaw needles of ice in bath and developer. Those were simple days, when lantern slides and negatives of moving subjects were alike made on one sensitive film – wet collodion – and varying 'speeds of plates' were almost unknown.

It was in November 1885 that Alfred and some of his friends, all pioneers of the amateur photographic movement in the county, founded the Herefordshire Photographic Society, one of the first such societies in the country. Their objective was 'to study photography and interchange ideas pertaining to the art of photography'. The first president of the newly-formed society was James Rankin M.P., later to become Sir James Rankin, Bart. The headquarters at that time was in Clarence House in Aubrey Street where occasional meetings were held. In 1888, when Alderman T. Blake of Ross became president, the Society held its first 'Field Day' in the Forest of Dean. Another, slightly later, involved a boat trip on the Wye from Ross to Monmouth. These enjoyable social outings have continued through to the present day with Club Evenings only in the winter.

These excursions were certainly not for the weak; as was described in the *Centenary Booklet* of the Society:

> Much physical exertion was required just to take part in these outings. The intrepid photographers of those days had to be strong and very fit as they had to carry half-a-hundredweight of equipment on their backs. Their cameras were large and heavy, they had glass plates on which to record their pictures ... a heavy tripod was a necessity together with a substantial focussing cover or hood.

At that time Alfred and all other photographers suffered from the problem which beset all early photographers – calculating the length of exposure needed for a successful picture. Standard exposure tables, depending on season, latitude, time of day and weather conditions were complex and highly inaccurate. The alternative was trial-and-error – expensive in materials and wasteful in time. Records had to be kept of successful exposures and these were used as a guide. Even then, there was no certain method of determining whether the exposure was one second or ten seconds out.

Watkins was one of the first people to appreciate that the main prerequisite of a good photograph was not the choice of camera, lens or plate, but the correct determination of the length of time that the plate was exposed to the light, and the right length of time that the negative was left in the developer, and he spent much time over the subsequent decades working on inventions to solve these problems.

In April 1890, Alfred published a paper in the *British Journal of Photography* on the subject of exposure, following his acquisition of a patent for a new invention – the actinometer. To tackle the problem of exposure, he had realised that what was needed was a method of measuring the relative intensity of light. He resolved this by inventing a machine which measured the intensity of the ambient light by counting the number of seconds that it took for a piece of sensitized paper to darken to the same tint as a fixed reference paper. This, together with a knowledge of the size of the aperture or diaphragm of the camera and the speed of the plate used, are the three factors which affect exposure. The aperture and the plate speed could be reduced to numerical values and the actinometer then produced a numerical value for the light.

Basically, the problem of exposure had been solved, and Alfred proceeded to design what was, in effect, a pocket calculator for determining exposure. This, the first exposure meter, consisted of an actinometer with revolving scales for the other two variables. Although it was described as being merely ingenious and commercially of little use, Alfred was convinced that his invention would allow any photographer, however inexperienced, to produce a correctly-exposed photograph. This, the Watkins Exposure Meter was, in the first instance, made by R. Field & Co., Instrument Makers of Suffolk Street in Birmingham. The first advertisement appeared in *The Photographic News Almanac* in 1892. According to

his son, Allen, in the first year of production he sold 1,400 Meters at a guinea each. By the middle of the 1890s the Meter was being made in four different patterns, ranging in price from 7s. 6d. for the Junior version to a guinea for the Standard one in a featherweight aluminium case.

The sales were obviously profitable and Alfred decided to set up his own business to manufacture and sell his exposure meters, and around 1900 he bought the 'goodwill, stock and book debts' of the Exposure Meter part of the business from R. Field & Co. An advertisement of 1901 stated:

> This change will bring both Technical and Commercial departments under the personal direction of the Inventor, and will, it is hoped, tend to strengthen and extend the almost personal relations existing between him and the thousands who use his methods.

Alfred started operating in a small shed-like building attached to the Imperial Flour Mills in Friar Street. This building was always simply known as The Meter Works. The business continued to be successful and Alfred soon produced a popular version – the famous Bee Meter (a name selected to suggest something small and highly efficient) – which, in its various forms, became the standard addition to every photographer's kit for almost half a century. Although the main business of The Meter Works was the making of photographic meters of various types, it also made some equipment associated with the baking of bread, including a patented Baker's Thermometer.

The Watkins Meter Company may well have been of greater interest, and thus more important, to Alfred than his major business enterprise in the Flour Mills. It operated with a staff of four – a manager and three young men who operated the lathes and put the instruments together. Alfred personally dealt with all the correspondence from other photographers and must have been responsible for most of the experimental work and the improved designs of specialist light meters, daylight developing tanks, thermometers, dark-room clocks and other equipment.

One question which was raised many times was – would the Watkins Meter work in other parts of the world where the light was of a different quality? Its total success was finally demonstrated to all when H.G. Ponting, the photographer who accompanied Scott's Antarctic Expedition in 1910, used a Watkins Meter to produce his amazing landscapes of this, at the time, almost totally unknown southern continent. On his return he wrote to Alfred to tell him that without the meter the work would have been impossible.

Following on from this impeccable reference, sales rapidly grew and became world-wide, instructions for the use of the meter being produced in most European languages. An order was even received from China; a meter was sent and the requisite half-a-crown was eventually received. Allen Watkins records this event as one of his father's most treasured experiences.

The second basic photographic problem that had to be resolved was that of development, and Alfred was determined to solve this by establishing a quantitative method which would produce precise results. His *Factorial Method of Development* was published in 1894. It was based on his own experiments and made use of what became known as the Watkins Factor. He established that to get a standard degree of contrast it was necessary to measure the time that it took from pouring the developer on the plate to the first appear-

Top: The Meter Works during the First World War when it was used for light industrial purposes
Bottom: The Bee Meter and advertisement cards

One of Alfred's cameras with case, now in Hereford City Museum
(Ken Hoverd, 1990)

A Watkins darkroom clock made at The Meter Works and a simple
pinhole camera, both in Hereford City Museum (Ken Hoverd, 1990)

ance of any trace of the image. Multiplying this time by the Factor would then give the precise development time required for perfect results. The Factor, of course, varied with the developer, and Alfred carried out many experiments to establish the correct figures to use in each case. The Watkins Meter Company eventually produced a darkroom clock and a factorial calculator to help photographers work out the correct development times.

To Alfred, photography had always been a technical subject in which the operator had to have a wide knowledge of the background principles in order to produce a quality picture. This did not mean that he must have expensive equipment – Alfred himself was the great improviser – but rather that he must understand the techniques and latest developments in what was then a scientific field of study for everyone who participated.

This was well illustrated in the tale his son told of his father sending a set of mounted photographs of a local estate to its owner. In his letter of thanks the owner made the rather unfortunate comment 'What a splendid camera you must have, Mr. Watkins!' Some time later the owner sent Watkins a brace of pheasants. 'What a splendid gun you must have, Sir John!' rejoined Alfred.

Most of Alfred's experiments in development were carried out in his dark room in the cellar of Vineyard Croft in Hampton Park. He did not rely on expensive equipment but made use of whatever came to hand. His son described the cellar steps at Vineyard Croft as a death-trap with the steepest steps he had ever seen. Apart from the darkroom, the rest of the cellar was full of shelves of apples which came from the large garden.

In 1894 Alfred Watkins was elected a member of the Royal Photographic Society; in 1910 he became a Fellow and in the same year he received their coveted Progress Medal for his extensive researches into photographic theory and practice.

Alfred's first camera was a cigar box with a pinhole for the lens, and he remained attached to this simple method of photography throughout his life, eventually marketing special pinhole lenses through the Meter Company. These had several sizes of pinhole and could be attached to ordinary cameras as a substitute for the glass lens. Such a camera has the advantage that it can work at any focus, can be used for wide or narrow angle views and gives an artistic texture to the photograph. The main disadvantage is the length of time needed for the exposure, which, with the slow plates then available, was measured in minutes rather than seconds. A further disadvantage was that, using the standard camera body of the period, the image could only be seen on the focussing screen in very bright light. Watkins solved this problem with typical simplicity. As he advised in his first book on photography, *The Watkins Manual of Exposure and Development*, published in 1894:

> Having levelled the stand and noted that the pinhole is opposite the centre of the plate, turn the camera round, and lifting the focus screen apply the eye to the pinhole and see if the view wanted is framed in the end of the camera. Then turn the camera round again for the pinhole to face the subject.

In 1898 the Herefordshire Photographic Society held its first public exhibition of members' work in the Public Library in Broad Street and, following this, membership gradually increased to about a hundred. As part of this event, several lectures were given and Alfred showed his considerable knowledge and expertise by talking on colour photography – at that time a very complex and time-consuming process. The exhibition continued this theme by including several examples of his early colour photographs.

Ladies were allowed to join the Photographic Society and, in a second exhibition during 1899, there was even a ladies competition. (It is interesting to note the differing attitude to the membership of ladies in the rather technical Photographic Society as compared with that in the more academic Woolhope Club, where lady membership was strongly opposed for many years). By 1900 Alfred Watkins was one of the vice-presidents of the Society which, in 1906, moved to new rooms at 76 Eign Street where they remained until 1914.

It was in 1907 that the 22nd Annual Meeting of the Photographic Convention of the United Kingdom was held in Hereford, as a mark of respect for Alfred Watkins, who was president of the Convention for that year. About 80 delegates from all over the country attended the six-day meeting, and Alfred gave the inaugural address. Delegates were greeted by members of a reception committee which included many of the most illustrious figures in the county. In the evening, after the official reception, there was a musical promenade and a display of the city charters and plate. The following week was full of excursions to local beauty spots including Weobley, Pembridge, Ledbury, Abbey Dore, Kilpeck and Bosbury. As president of the Convention, Alfred and his wife held an 'At Home' at Vineyard Croft for all the delegates. Apart from the usual hospitality, the Watkins also offered their visitors boating and punting on the Wye!

The programme booklet contained several articles of local interest including one by Alfred on Hereford in which he described some of the historic buildings that delegates could visit during their stay. Other articles included one by the Dean entitled *Notes on Hereford Cathedral* and one by Ella Mary Leather (who five years later was to have her book *Folklore of Herefordshire* published by Jakeman and Carver of Hereford) about the villages of Weobley and Pembridge.

A comprehensive work on photography was lacking in the early 20th century, and so in 1910 Constable and Co. asked Alfred if he would be prepared to write one. The result, *Photography: its Principles and Applications,* was published in 1911 and rapidly became the standard reference book, even containing a chapter on colour photography, the coloured frontispiece being a garden scene taken from an autochrome by Alfred himself. This process, invented by Lumière of Lyons, had only been issued commercially in 1907 so was still very new and exciting. A review of the book, published in the *Morning Post*, concluded that 'There are few photographers of experience who will not be of opinion that the conclusions and experiences of Mr. Watkins are worth a library of compiled textbooks'.

Alfred also took an early interest in the cinema and went to Chester in 1890 to see a demonstration by Mr. Friese Green, the inventor of the ciné projector and the first person to take and produce a series of negatives on a continuous band of celluloid film. This, the first moving film picture ever produced, featured a human

It was in May 1932, when ploughing a field at Olchon Court on the slopes of the Black Mountains, that a large stone was encountered. On lifting the stone a small cist was revealed which contained a male skeleton, a beaker and an arrowhead. On probing the ground around this cist another was disclosed nearby, also with a skeleton and beaker. The burials were of Early Bronze Age date. Alfred, then 76 years old, took all the site photographs and helped with the removal of the first cist and its contents to Hereford Museum, where they are on display from time to time.

Top right: Before finding the second cist
Bottom right: The two cists when opened
Below: The beaker from the first cist

hand opening and shutting. In later life, Alfred possessed a hand-turned ciné camera, and some 35mm films, made by him of events in Hereford, survive and are now stored in the archives of the British Film Institute. These films include Kitchener's recruits marching past the Hereford Eye Hospital in 1914, and some of the first motorcycle trials which took place on Stockley Hill.

In 1907 Walter Pilley, a friend of Alfred, was elected president of the Photographic Society, a position he held until about 1912, when he was succeeded by Alfred himself. It was during this year that the first lady, a Miss Gladstone, was elected to the council of the society. Although meetings continued to be held during the First World War this was obviously a difficult period, and membership gradually dropped to about 20. It is evident that Alfred was not satisfied with the general affairs of the Society, and in 1921 he wrote to the council apologising for his non-attendance at their meeting due to illness and resigning as president. He said that he was willing to continue as a member and do what he could in the interests of the Society 'providing the Society was completely reorganised'.

This was apparently agreed to, and Sir John Arkwright was elected president with Godfrey Davies acting as both secretary and treasurer. At that time Davies was the youngest member of the society and indeed had only joined in 1919. The Society was also in debt and several fund-raising efforts were held. The 1920s continued to be difficult years and the society again suffered from falling numbers. It eventually folded and all activities were suspended in 1927.

Alfred was never to know that the society, which he had helped to form, was to be reborn in 1937 some two years after his death. Despite the Second World War, membership increased steadily and, contrary to all expectations, this became one of the most successful periods in the whole of the Society's history. In 1943, when wartime restrictions were at their peak, it was decided that the Society would arrange a series of lectures to be called The Alfred Watkins Memorial Lectures, with the objects of 'keeping alive the memory of that pioneer worker and of encouraging still further development of photography in every sphere'.

The inaugural lecture, held in the Town Hall on 23 July 1943, was given by F.J. Mortimer, who had been editor of *The Amateur Photographer* for almost forty years. His subject was topical – 'Photography's Part in the War' – and attracted an audience of some four hundred people. During the lecture he disclosed that film processing in the R.A.F. was carried out entirely by the time and temperature method invented by Watkins.

The second memorial lecture was held later in the same year, on 14 October. It was given by Donald McMaster, the managing director of the British division of Kodak and president of the Royal Photographic Society. His subject – 'The Next Decade in Photography' – forecast the appearance of cheap, small, film cameras with synchronised flash – effectively the sort of cameras which were used by most people until very recently. After his lecture Mr. McMaster opened the first Anglo-American Salon of Photography in the city library, which drew over a thousand visitors. When, some time later, Mr. McMaster returned to America in overall charge of Kodak, he was responsible for the addition of a separate section devoted to the inventions of Alfred Watkins in their museum of photography, at George Eastman House in New York.

Alfred was not just a technical expert; he also had a true sense of composition. His son, Allen, could not have put it better when he said of his father that 'his love of Herefordshire came out in his photographs'. Allen emphasized this in a letter to the *Hereford Times* shortly after the centenary of his father's birth, when he wrote:

> Driving his steam car he would stop suddenly in the middle of nowhere and exclaim "Just look at that group of Hereford cows with the old stone bridge over the brook in the foreground: what a picture. I must get a negative of that at once. The evening side-light will be just right." And out would come his camera.

'Alfred Watkins loved his native city and had its interest ever at heart.' So wrote George Marshall in the long obituary published in the *Hereford Times* on Saturday 13 April 1935. It was this affection, coupled with the regular use of his camera to record the changes which were taking place in the city down to the most minute detail, which made him one of the most important observers of his period. Although he regularly examined excavations and trenches in the city he was seldom involved in formal archaeological work, being content to watch and record the efforts of others. He also examined historic buildings, especially if they were under threat, and although he did not produce many formal drawings, he described and photographed them and thus produced a record which is regularly used today. He combined the rare ability, which is always the trademark of the great archaeologist, of being able to interpret the complexities of buildings, trench sections, and other man-made features, with a capacity to enthral an audience with his findings.

The Meter Company in Friar Street continued to produce a wide variety of equipment and during the First World War the equipment was used for light engineering. However, once the war was over Alfred went back to producing photographic equipment, eventually with Mr. W.H. McKaig as manager, and the business continued successfully until his death.

Allen Watkins recounts a tragic end to the Meter Company:

> On my father's death, he bequeathed the business to the man who had been his constant companion and helper in his closing years [Mr. McKaig]. The latter very soon afterwards was attacked by cancer and died after an awful year of suffering borne with extraordinary good humour and bravery. He, in turn, left the business to his nephew, an undeveloped lad who was quite unfit for real responsibility. Things went wrong with the poor lad, and he was found hanging by the neck with a chair kicked from under him in the Meter Works shed.

Alfred – perhaps unsurprisingly – was much more concerned about what would happen to his photographic equipment, slides and negatives, and his large collection of books, after his death than with the rest of his estate. His relatively short will (only two pages long), dated December 1930, includes explicit instructions to settle this matter. He appointed his son Allen, his daughter

Marion and local solicitor, Harold Gwynne James, as executors and trustees of his estate. There is no indication in the will that the Meter Works business was bequeathed to Mr. McKaig, so there was presumably a private arrangement that McKaig should continue to run the business. However, Alfred did bequeath to 'William Henry McKaig [shown as McKay in the will], my Manager at the Meter Works, all my photographic cameras and lenses all my lantern apparatus lantern slides and photographic negatives'. Following McKaig's death the photographic negatives and prints, consisting of some 3,500 items, were obtained by Hereford Library, where they remain. Much of Alfred's photographic equipment eventually passed to Hereford Museum and is regularly on display.

Alfred also left 'all my books photographs appliances microscope and slides and other effects of a personal nature to me' equally between his wife and children subject to the Trustees donating to Hereford Free Library one or two of his 'collections of Books relating to Archaeology, Bee-keeping and Photography (Historical)'. Finally he left some money to various relatives, and the balance of his estate was then divided between his son and daughter subject to a life interest in favour of his wife.

Alfred Watkins (1855-1935)

Gallery

A street scene in Wigmore around 1895

Croft Farm at Wyson, half a mile north-west of Brimfield, is of 17th-century date with square panelling. It faces a weather-boarded barn.

Cottage at Brimfield

Pembridge. Looking westwards along West Street in 1901.
The 16th-century house with its prominent upper storey obviously attracted Alfred's attention

Pembridge, looking east from the western edge of this quiet village, with a small flock of sheep being shepherded through the main street. The jettied white house on the left can also be seen in the distance in the photograph on the opposite page.

Pembridge. The old lodging house, which has since been demolished.

Weobley. Church Lane, with a carefully posed artist.

Weobley. The north side of the High Street with the Unicorn Inn in the middle distance.

Weobley. Broad Street looking towards St. Peter and St. Paul's church with its commanding spire. Central to the photograph, in Bell Square, is the Red Lion Inn, its fine timberwork covered in render when this photograph was taken.

Eardisland Turnpike. Two turnpikes are recorded at Eardisland; as no trace remains of either, it is not clear whether this is the Broad Bridge or the Legion Cross Turnpike.

Brookside Cottage, a 16th-century, and later, timber-framed house near the brook at Mansell Lacy in 1924. The narrow studding would have been expensive and is of high quality. It shows a degree of affluence and is particularly impressive in a rural setting.

The rope stall, Hereford Cattle Market

Throughout Alfred's lifetime, regular visits of various circuses caused excitement in Hereford, not least when animals were paraded through the streets and allowed to bathe in the river – as camels and elephants are doing here in 1899. They were part of Barnum & Bailey's Circus, advertised as 'The Greatest Show on Earth'

Looking west along Hereford's High Town at night.
The clock on the Butter Market shines well and All Saints Church stands high in the background.
Judging the exposure time must have been very difficult.

Looking across the Close towards Hereford Cathedral on a snowy day. The photograph is taken from the corner of the Close next to St. John Street, where the statue of Sir Edward Elgar, Alfred's contemporary, now stands.

Roaring Meg, the 'toss-pot' that caused much damage towards the end of the Civil War, both at Goodrich and Raglan Castles, languished for many years in Hereford, standing on its muzzle at the corner of Bridge Street and Gwynne Street. It was eventually 'rescued' and moved to Castle Green, as shown in this photograph. A later move to the then Churchill Gardens Museum did not last very long. It now stands resplendent, with a completely new carriage, in the courtyard of Goodrich Castle, where it originally caused so much damage.

The Preaching Cross in the Blackfriars monastery grounds, showing vegetable gardens at the rear of Coningsby Hospital, Hereford. The monastery was originally established in Portfields, the monks being granted this site in 1319. Following the Dissolution, the site and buildings were granted to John Scudamore of Wilton. Some ruins of the monastery still stand, but much of the area is now landscaped gardens, and the land beyond built up.

Some of the residents seated outside Coningsby Hospital in Widemarsh Street, Hereford. It was founded in 1614 by Sir Thomas Coningsby for poor old soldiers or mariners of at least three years' service in the wars or at sea, or serving men of seven years' service. Its residents included a corporal, chaplain and ten servitors. The building takes the form of a quadrangle with 12 apartments, a chapel and a hall. The Coningsby Arms are prominent above the entrance.

Price's Almhouses or Hospital, on the northern side of Whitecross Road in Hereford, was founded in 1665 by Mr. William Price,
alderman of London, for 12 aged men, freemen of the city being preferred. The long range includes a chapel at the eastern end.
Alfred's photographs of historic buildings often included carefully posed people.

A section of Hereford City Wall in Gunners' Lane looking north. The building in the background has since been demolished and the Victoria Street section of the Inner Relief Road is on the opposite side of the wall.

The ivy-clad bastion tower on the Hereford City Wall, one of the two that survive. Although the lean-to shed has been demolished and the ivy removed, it is still rather hidden next to the Greyfriars surgery off St. Nicholas Street, but it is easily seen from the approach to Greyfriars Bridge. Alfred proposed an historical sequence to the defences that continues to be used today.

Alfred was there to record the demolition in the late 19th century of a rather fine stretch of the Hereford City Wall, just to the west of Widemarsh Street, to make way for a brand new building – the Wellington Arms, now called JDs.

In his own way, watercolourist David Cox (1783-1859) recorded the countryside around Hereford as faithfully as Alfred did. His iconic landscape 'The Lugg Meadows, nr. Hereford' was painted from a vantage point near this cottage at Baynton Wood while he was living there *c.*1817.

Boating on the river Lugg at Lugwardine with the river meadows in the background

A thatched cottage at Lugwardine. Even in Alfred's time many houses lacked the light for indoor reading, and this sight would not have been uncommon.

Hovels on Broadmoor Common, Woolhope, around 1890

A late 19th-century view of Fownhope. The two simple thatched cottages on the left have been demolished. One of them was at one time the communal wash house.

Poor houses known as The Barracks at Kingsthorne

The church of St. Dubricius at Hentland, some ten miles south of Hereford, was built in around 1300.
The west tower was added in the 14th century.

Clodock Mill on the river Monnow with its impressive large iron waterwheel, made at Leominster in 1868. The mill is still in good order today.

Cusop Dingle. The building on the left is the early 19th-century Cusop Mill, now a private house.
The photograph may well have been taken on one of Alfred's visits to the excavations at Craswall Priory.

Several types of willow (called osiers) have long flexible branches
which when stripped are used in basket making.

The pedlar outside Derndale, a 17th-century farmhouse in
Canon Pyon, in 1918

'The organ man'. Alfred may well have photographed the same organ grinder that local artist Brian Hatton drew in the mid-1890s.
Both photograph and drawing are now in Hereford Library and Museum.

'His first cigarette', a country scene photographed in 1903

Index

Index of illustrations

Also from Logaston Press

The Dovecotes and Pigeon Houses of Herefordshire
by Robert Walker
Paperback, 200 pages, 8 colour and 160 black & white images
ISBN 978 1906663 49 0 £12.95

The dovecote at Garway is the earliest-dated dovecote in Britain, and it is just one of the 300 dovecotes and pigeon houses covered in this book. They include substantial octagonal brick structures and vernacular timber-framed edifices, accommodation for pigeons built into eaves, gables, and even the occasional chimney or belfry. This is a completely fresh survey of Herefordshire's dovecotes and pigeon houses, but includes many of Alfred Watkins' and Israel Cohen's photographs of the late 1800s and 1950s, records of dovecotes that no longer exist. Robert Walker shows that pigeons could not have been a staple winter food for the lord of the manor, and that it was the young birds, or squabs, that provided a delicacy at certain times of the year.

Royalist, but ... Herefordshire in the English Civil War, 1640-51
by David Ross
Paperback, 208 pages, 45 b/w illustrations
ISBN 978 1906663 63 6 £12.95

On the eve of the Civil War in 1642, Herefordshire's leading families were all, to a greater or lesser extent, for the King – with the one notable exception of the Harleys at Brampton Bryan. As a result, Herefordshire was seen as a recruiting ground by Royalist military commanders, and as rather backward by some on the Parliamentary side. But once war had broken out with all its consequences, the majority were rather lukewarm in their support for the King. David Ross has a deep knowledge of this period which he uses with skill to craft a vivid picture of Herefordshire's inhabitants in these years of turmoil.

Herefordshire Past & Present, An Aerial View
by Chris Musson and Ruth E. Richardson
Paperback: 112 pages, 110 colour and 20 black & white photos and drawings
ISBN: 978 1904396 20 8 £14.95

In these photographs it is possible to see evidence of a Bronze Age circle, of Iron Age farms and settlements, of medieval mills and settlements. The book also allows one to appreciate the line of transport networks, from the Roman crossing of the Wye near Kenchester, through tramroads, canals and railways to modern bypasses. Thumbnail sketches help explain pictures of cropmarks at Magnis, rabbit warren farming at Willey, the Grandmontine Priory at Craswall, the multiple bailey system at Kingsland Castle and the development of Longtown. There are also startling photos of the major towns which are such a distinctive feature of the county.

Roses round the door? Rural images, realities & responses: Herefordshire, 1830s-1930s
by Tim Ward
Paperback, 168 pages, 135 b/w illustrations
ISBN 978 1906663 22 3 £12.95

Tim Ward's collection of postcards includes many images of Herefordshire's past rural life: harvesting and hop-picking, cidermaking and cattle breeding, blacksmiths, beekeepers and basketmakers. Behind these photographs, carefully posed as most of them had to be for the slow business of early photography, were the working lives of men and women – and many of those lives were a hard struggle, however picturesque the scenes seem to be. Life was far from a 'roses round the door' country idyll. This book is made up of a combination of those images and the stories behind the pictures. For, dispossessed by the Enclosure Acts that took common land from rural people and forced them into miserable working and living conditions, Herefordshire's agricultural labourers eventually found a voice, with the formation, from 1871, of a succession of farmworkers' unions. Tim Ward charts the history of the unions, the strong characters who founded them, including Thomas Strange, William Gibson Ward, Joseph Arch and Sidney Box, and what became of their attempts to bring about change.

Herefordshire Place-Names
by Bruce Coplestone-Crow
Paperback, 268 pages, 7 maps
ISBN 978 1906663 21 6 £12.95

This book seeks to explain the place-names of Herefordshire — not just those of the major settlements, but also of districts, hamlets and even old farmsteads. For each entry all the known versions of the name that have been used in documents down the ages are set out, these helping indicate how the name has reached what it is today, and the form in which it started life. The meanings are given, and there is often additional information about the family which may have lent its name to the place, why a name has changed over time or concerning old charter bounds. At the beginning of the book the author has used his considerable knowledge to set out in some detail the origins for the old district names within Herefordshire, many of which (such as Archenfield, Leen, Lyde, Maund and Straddle) are a component of many current place-names.

You're not from round here, are you? An A-Z of Proper People and People from Off
by Roger Kite with drawings by Ken Hutchinson
Paperback, 60 pages, 35 b/w drawings
ISBN: 978 1906663 03 2 £4.95

D is for Doing Things. A common complaint from proper people about people from off is that they simply don't know how to do things. Now clearly there are lots of things they do know how to do, such as managing off-shore investments or knowing which golf club to use. So what are proper people getting at? What they mean is that your typical person from off is of no use to them at all: he has no idea how to build a fence, trouse a hedge, deliver a calf, work a sheepdog, worm a horse, hang a gate, or do anything else remotely useful to a proper person. So, grim though it is, the question has to be asked: just what are people from off for?